# DIGITAL
# BANKING

# TIPS

## Practical Ideas for Disruptors

# TOLGA TAVLAS

# Praise for Digital Banking Tips

"Tolga's blog is my go-to site for a sharp, incisive and up to date perspective on a changing digital world in the retail banking market..." **Julia O'Hegarty, Programme Director, Efma**

"Digital Banking seen from practical perspective. Illuminating tips based on experience and observation of real events...!" **Giuseppe Servillo, Senior Manager at Accenture Strategy**

"Tolga gives a profound insight of key digital topics affecting the financial industry with tremendous impact. His series of tips provide very useful and executable information and solutions in a clear, pragmatic, and compact way..." **Raphael König and Julia Pallanitsch, (ERGO Insurance Group)**

Great observations and I fully agree that(...)digital banking should be a joint effort of various groups, such as technology, marketing, branding and channel management." **Makoto Shibata Head of Global Innovation, The Bank of Tokyo-Mitsubishi UFJ**

From one of the most brilliant banking executives, the perfect toolbox for redesigning your organization around digital. (...)Tolga distils his experience for any bank that is facing the challenge of turning their digital agenda into more than a buzzword." **Paolo Barbesino, First VP, Head of Digital - CEE Retail at UniCredit Bank Austria AG**

Tolga Tavlas has a lot of expertise and thinks hard about sensible and workable strategies for dealing with fraud risks in a fast-changing environment." **Michael Levi, Professor of Criminology at Cardiff University**

# DIGITAL BANKING

# TIPS

## Practical Ideas for Disruptors

# TOLGA TAVLAS

**DIGITAL BANKING TIPS:** Copyright © January 2016

By: Tolga Tavlas

DBT: Vienna Austria

Editor and interior design by: Melissa Scott

Melissa@TheWriterLab.com

For more information contact:

TOLGA@DIGITALBANKINGTIPS.COM

Or visit the author's website at:

WWW.DIGITALBANKINGTIPS.COM

ISBN-13: 978-1514255711

ISBN-10: 1514255715

Second Edition published by DBT: November 2015

To My wife, Günin, and My Little Monkey,
Defne – I love you so much ☺

# CONTENTS

What does a digital banking leader have in common with a cruise boat captain? They both need to be multi-talented and nearly all-knowing superstars to steer their ships to success.

When you're a ship's captain it's not nearly enough to just take your boat from point A to point B. While doing so, you also need to also keep all the myriads of machinery running at peak performance. You need to keep your staff working in harmony, and you need to engage with your passengers while working hard to keep them safe. And after all of that, if your passengers don't return for their next cruise vacation—you will have failed.

Likewise, digital banking can function similarly. Aside from general banking savvy, it also requires a mastery of digital channel technologies, security, ease of use, Omni channel integration, cross-functional leadership, motivated staff and buy-in across the board. At the same time, you need to engage with your customers as individuals, transforming them into raving fans, loyal users and lucrative clients.

That's not all. A digital banking leader also needs to combine the strategic with the practical in order to avoid getting stuck in analysis paralysis and over engineering. You need to combine the strategic vision of where you want to be in five years, with a sound judgment of what is feasibly right for building revenue and profits with what you have, and given what your target market is ready to adopt.

And just like a ship's captain surrounded by sirens leading him or her off course, a digital banker is pursued by vendors with their own agenda—no matter how mature or nascent their product is. Meanwhile, Fraudsters want to empty your ship's hold with a smile.

How about those icebergs that threaten to sink ships? Just like that, technical risks are seemingly all around, threatening to blow a hole in your vault.

Here to help you navigate these waters safely and swiftly is Tolga Tavlas with his brilliant tips found in this book. Tolga's tips provide priceless and practical guidance for digital bankers drawing on his seventeen-plus years of leadership experience on the front lines of digital innovation at multiple banks in multiple countries. This is the kind of practical

## Tolga Tavlas

know-how you can't learn in school, nor can you get it from theory books or vendor whitepapers.

Well written and with a great dose of humor, Tolga's tips are sure to stimulate creative discussion for your institution's most critical journey into the digital realm. Don't leave the harbor without this compass in your pocket.

**Akin Arikan**

**Author of "Multichannel Marketing: Metrics and Methods for On - and Offline success."**

# INTRODUCTION

## Who should read this book?

If your financial institution has been in business for a while, making the move to digital banking could be the most challenging thing you've had to deal with in a long time. You might have a pretty good idea of where you want to end up, but right now the path to get there is hidden behind a fog of uncertainty. Fortunately you've picked up this guide, filled with advice from those who've travelled that same path before!

Perhaps you are in a position to offer services to a financial institution that offers digital banking? This book can help you understand what those companies need, and how you can package your products in a way that will help them move their business forward. There are limitless opportunities for GSM (Telecom) operators, software developers, and value-added service providers to further cultivate this segment of their market.

As of today, there are nearly three billion people using the internet, but implementation of digital banking services and embracing of digital banking practices has remained inconsistent. Occasionally there are technical reasons—if a system is difficult to learn or onerous to operate, why use that rather than visiting your local branch with its friendly service and (more importantly) free coffee?

Some customers may worry about the security of their money and personal information. While younger customers (the ones you want to attract today in the hopes of making them lifelong patrons) love digital banking and expect it to be available, preferably as an app on their phones. This younger generation will also expect to have access to free Wi-Fi when visiting their local branch. Longstanding customers may be more cautious about using new technology and hesitant to give up the personal service they've come to expect.

You may even have frontline staff that are unwilling to promote digital banking services because they are concerned about their own job security or are unwilling to learn new skills. Ask any manager how much they enjoy hearing, "this is the way we've always done it!" After their exaggerated eye roll, you will doubtless be regaled with entertaining stories about staff that was less than excited about implementing a new procedure.

Developing a digital banking presence is a daunting task, especially when you consider the financial resources and public education needed to achieve telephone, online, or mobile banking capabilities. Where to start? That's where this book comes in. It's a quick and easy read, the tips are simple to implement, and you may even find a little banking humor to help you through the process.

If your company has offered digital banking services in the past, this book can help you build that part of your business by assisting with areas such as:

> **New Users:** How can you best encourage your existing customers to adopt online banking?

> **Increased Usage:** How can you get your customers to take advantage of the full range of digital services you provide?

> **Improved Systems:** Technology changes with remarkable speed, and users are always looking for ways to make their lives easier and their banking more secure. As the saying goes, "Life moves pretty fast …"

> **Multi-Channel Business Needs:** How can you seamlessly incorporate your digital

banking services with your business model?

➢ **Employee Buy-In:** How can you get your frontline staff to embrace systems they may view as replacing … frontline staff?

➢ **Understanding Your System:** Most importantly, you need to feel comfortable with digital banking and have a strong sense of where the market is going, what's working, and what isn't.

## What does "Digital Banking" even mean?

The phrase "Digital Banking" has different meanings for different people. It may refer to the current state or future of banking, and it could be where we are now or the level of service that we want to reach. I always love simplicity so I have used a simple definition: "**providing banking/financial services through self-service channels with limited or no branch support.**" Internet and mobile banking services are the most crucial elements of Digital Banking, but they should also be supported by Contact Centers, ATMs, Notification Services and Branches.

There are other books written on this subject, but what is missing is an execution guide. We need a quick and dirty manual that tells us how to implement digital banking services. This is a short --

to the point, and action-oriented (rather than theoretical) book. My motivation is to share with and learn from others, and then use this knowledge as a base to create new tips and share again!

Innovation is certainly required, but it's not always about technology. Rather, it is about using what you already have in different ways to create a change. Not every bank or financial institution has huge resources and leadership that supports digital transformation, or fully engaged employees with a digital mindset. So the idea is to provide useful tips that you can execute easily in the current environment of your company - with or without some investments.

Since I promised to provide simple and easy to read material, I will share simple tips in the form of a clear and easy to use format. These tips have already been shared with tens of thousands professionals all over the world in my blog and fine-tuned for this book in light of reader's feedback. The huge response to these tips has encouraged me to turn my blog into a book and extend the scope. The tips are categorized in four groups:

> **Growing Fast:** Getting more clients on board and convincing them to use Digital Banking.

- ➢ **Generating Revenue:** Creating leads and sales for financial products, preparing user journeys and customer interactions.

- ➢ **Security:** Both client side and bank side (preventive, monitoring, and after incident.)

- ➢ **360 Degree Landscape:** Social media, ATMs, kiosks, other stakeholders, and compliance, legal teams, location-based services, Big Data, and many others...

Digital banking is the future of financial institutions. This book will help you get there in simple, actionable steps. Whatever your position in your company, whether you're enthusiastic about sailing forward, or still uncertain about stepping off the dock, let's take this journey together.

## What Kind of Tips are we talking about?

Here's a short example of a simple Digital Banking Tip:

*It sounds a little bit strange, but checking out the system error messages that a customer gets could produce quite interesting results and leads.*

*Let me explain how this is possible. If a customer gets such a message it means she/he wants to do something but we do not allow this action for a valid reason. Some examples of such messages are:*

*"insufficient funds, over the limit transactions, blocked password, your electric bill is not paid or cannot be paid, etc." It is very easy to find out how many clients receive such messages each and every day.*

*So let's go into more detail for the error message, "insufficient funds." Who gets this message and why? Most likely a customer who would like to perform a money transfer or purchase a product. Well, some of the clients who receive such messages could also be eligible for a loan offering and this could be an excellent opportunity to sell the credit product to the client at the moment of need. Of course, some propensity model work with your customer relationship management, or at least some profiling may give you a clue who could be eligible for such an offer. It works quite well, I can tell you this from first hand experience! Not necessarily for online banking only, but also for ATMs and Contact Centers too.*

*We discovered this by chance when we experienced a system interruption and we had to check how many clients were influenced. Considering that there were millions of active users (thank God only a small percent of them were trying to access the system at the time of the interruption - but even so it was a big number!), it was quite a tiring and a boring task. So, adversity triggered the intelligence - and the idea came to our minds. We decided to give it a try and organized a pilot program. We were completely amazed with the results!*

*Most of the time, micro loans would be a good and simple product to sell at such an occurrence.*

If you find this interesting, go ahead – there are many others in this book!

## CHAPTER 1

## TIP ONE: ACCESSIBILITY AND ENGAGEMENT

**"The purpose of a business is to create a customer."** *Peter Drucker*

In theory, accessibility is always there - at the end of the day, clients can go to the branch to get a password, or fill out many fields of the online forms etc. However in practice, clients may not like visiting branches (come on guys, we're talking about digital banking clients - they are not branch lovers!) or they may not fully understand what we ask for in our online forms. In addition, it should also be noted that as digital channels fully rely on data - any quality issue will be turned into an accessibility issue too. As a result, the number of active online users is far fewer than the total number of clients interested in using digital channels. So if the growth is planned, all obstacles in front of accessibility should be removed. But how?

In most countries, due to regulations and traditional banking practices, the **Branch** is the first point of contact with the customer. Ideally, digital banking customers should have nothing to do with the branch, but when concerning new account openings, the branch is the place to go - for most countries. (For sure, there are some fantastic ways to open an account without going to the branch, like using digital signatures or making money transfers from another bank, etc. but not very common and valid for most.) There are two good ways of utilizing the branch for digital banking: **auto-on boarding** and **obtaining client data**. As the name implies, auto-on boarding means that having digital banking access should be part of the account opening process. In addition, alert and reminder services should be introduced to the client as well. The other critical point is obtaining the client's valid information, which is required for legal and business reasons. Getting contact information and validating it especially has tremendous benefits. Motivating branches for this purpose is a requirement and we will go into further detail in upcoming tips.

Another interesting channel for accessibility is **ATMs**, which can be used for application - getting passwords - changing GSM numbers and gaining client approval for some actions (as second factor). I think it is also worthwhile to note that even if not very common, there are some ATMs with keyboard access too, which gives more flexibility in terms of services provided. (Please use with caution – as potential customers waiting in the queue may not like the idea of someone at the machine for a long time.) Another way ATMs can be useful is by utilizing their idle screens to advertise the benefits of digital banking with an "apply now" call to action.

The **Call Center**, from password distribution/recovery to data update, (depending on the skill set and FTE available) is another critical contributor. One very important component of Call Center usage is automation and security. The accessibility processes should be designed with this in mind. Agents accessing critical data may create internal fraud risks (this is a rising trend of online banking fraud), that is why data masking and a "need to know basis" of data access are also required.

And very best of all, for sure, is **Web based Application** for Digital Banking Accessibility for both new password and password recovery. In practice, just a few fields with a couple of validations (should take around a minute) can do the job very effectively. Most of the users would either be, clients who are working for your bank but do not have Digital Banking Access, or users with Digital Banking Access but with lost/blocked passwords. There are many successful examples for using such Digital Banking Application forms, most of them utilizing **Credit/Debit Card Number & Pin** (but some of the banks do not want this due to PCI DSS regulations of Card Providers) or Data Only fields. The form should be very short and to the point. Otherwise, (according to independent surveys) for every second page - almost 50% of users are lost. A simple calculation says that, only 12.5 of 100 users will begin a four page application form and actually complete it. The online digital banking form should also be used by the kiosks at the branches too.

Here's your checklist to improve your Digital Banking Accessibility and Engagement:

1. Which credentials are used to log-in into the Digital banking?

2. On-boarding process: How customers enroll to the internet / mobile banking - which channels are used for application and which channel is dominant? (Branch, Web, ATM or Call Center)

3. Are any online application forms used? If so, which fields exist in the application form and how much time does it take for a typical client to complete?

4. How long does it take to become a Digital Banking client? Is there any precondition or requirement? If so, what is it?

5. Is there an auto on-boarding program used at branches? How is a newly acquired client informed about the Digital Banking process?

6. Has there ever been a propensity model

worked before? If so, what was done and what was achieved?

7. What kind of contracts, fliers, forms and documentation are used for Digital Banking at branches?

8. Is there a regular/ongoing campaign or promotion informing activities for Digital Banking? If so, who is managing it? Is it centrally or locally coordinated? Has a budget been allocated for this purpose?

9. What motivations are used for both the client and the bank side for migration to Digital Channels? What is in it for them? (the incentives schemes?)

10. Are there any packages or bundles? Do these include multi-channel services?

11. Are there any special internet / mobile migration programs ongoing at any level?

12. Do you have any Direct Sales force? If so, what are they doing and how is their performance? Do they sell internet & Mobile?

13. Which "quick wins" have you observed by now? What can be done for seamless customer experience across the channels?

14. Which analytics are used or planned to be used? And how will this contribute to the success of the engagement?

15. Have there been any recent software purchases which have not deployed yet? Likewise, what are the ongoing IT projects related with Customer Engagement? If so when and what will they deliver?

16. Has application funnel been monitored? How many clients wanted to apply for the password and how many of them successfully got it?

17. Which obstacles exist against the easy migration of clients to Digital Channels and what can be done to overcome them?

If you want to increase your Digital Banking users and enjoy all the benefits Digital Channels can provide, Accessibility and Engagement are the two most essential components that should be crafted well, and regularly maintained.

## IN A NUTSHELL

Accessibility is very critical part of providing Digital Banking service. Even if you have the best online/mobile banking application - without accessibility, it has no use.

## CHAPTER 2

## TIP TWO: REMOVING BARRIERS

"Exceed your customer's expectations. If you do, they'll come back over and over. Give them what they want - and a little more." *Sam Walton*

**USER IDs and PASSWORDs** are the most commonly used credentials for accessing Digital Banking, so we need to deliver them to the customers who would like to use our online or mobile banking services. In order to facilitate this, there are flows and processes we've created that we think are pretty secure and easy to use. Well... our clients may not agree with this - what looks simple to us, may be seen as burdensome. We are losing too many clients in the digital banking application processes. Also, when the OTP (one time password) tools and other requirements come into play, everything becomes even more difficult.

Our clients' digital banking needs are NOT unique. Some may like to use all the functions (this is what we want too,) but others might only use it for inquiry only, or prefer to disable risky transactions. That means **FULL     USE, LIMITED     USE** and **INQUIRY ONLY USE** of digital banking channels are possible. Then we can ask ourselves, should we deploy the same level of security for different types of usage? Or we might differentiate our security settings / procedures depending on the Usage type so that we may turn this into our advantage at the time of the on boarding, by making minimum required security checks.

We can increase your Digital Banking client base by using any or all of the following three tools:

> ➢ Penetration

> ➢ Acquisition

> ➢ Re-activation

In my opinion each and every one of these three deserves a strong focus and understanding, because when used well, they can create miracles. If we target new clients from our bank's database (i.e. those who are not using digital banking) – this is **PENETRATION.** If we plan to gain new clients from our competitors or persuade some unbanked people (which is like starting to run, before learning to walk) to use our digital banking – this is **ACQUSITION.** If we can convince our inactive (churned or dormant) ex-clients, to use our digital banking – this is **RE-ACTIVATION.** (If we do not care about any of them, this may be called EARLY RETIREMENT or PRE-MATURE TERMINATION of our employment contract with the bank!)

Penetration and Re-activation are relatively easy, if we can deliver the User ID and Password to the client. The very basic question is what does it take to be a Digital Banking client? What do we ask our clients during the application process? Less is better. Sure there are rules, regulations, security and legal issues that are all on the table, but still this does not change the fact that less is better. How can we simplify the Login Processes on the basis of providing different types of access levels?

Don't get me wrong, of course "Full Use" should be the target. We are digital banking professionals with the ultimate target of migrating every banking transaction and customer online. At the same time, as of now most banks and their clients experience some kind of transformation. There are still a significant number of customers who have never used digital channels. We should have them on board first. ("First we need to convince them to come to the temple, then teach them how to pray!") If our offerings together with convenience are strong enough – they will never leave the digital world.

Let's think about USER IDs. Do you provide the user ID or ask the client to set up a user ID? It is a very good idea to use the information that is already known by the client and already stored in your bank's database; something like their Citizenship ID, Social Security number, Customer Number or even GSM Number. Also, you can let the client choose some custom IDs – under the standards you set up (would you like to use user IDs given by Facebook or Twitter? How about ZD789389@gmail.com email address?!) Human beings have a strong orientation to forget things they do not understand or like (this is how politicians survive!) User IDs are no exception. Let them choose what they want…

How about Passwords? You should be stricter with the subject of Passwords for sure. At the same time, rather than blindly accepting what the security guys say – you might have to work on some Password Usability. Banks are dealing with money, so expecting that they will employ the same security standards with Social Media accounts or other service providers is absurd. However, this doesn't mean that we have to force our clients to use impossible to remember passwords ($#35AbD2). It is also worthwhile to note that password recovery mechanisms and having the capability of providing new passwords in less than sixty seconds, are the main backups of your growth.

In my opinion, the best solution would be to completely eradicate the use of Passwords and User IDs. There are excellent blog posts, books and articles on this very subject, but this will take some time for the general market to mature. So passwords will be with us awhile longer and it is worth learning how to manage them!

The next tip will be about Card Logins, which eliminates the need for Digital Banking User IDs & Passwords and very effectively used by many banks.

### IN A NUTSHELL

There are still a significant number of customers who have never used digital channels. We should have them on board first. If our offerings together with convenience are strong enough – they will never leave the digital world.

## CHAPTER 3

## TIP THREE: CREDIT/DEBIT CARDS AS ACCESS KEYS

**"When I was young, people lived from paycheck to paycheck. Today, it seems like they live from credit card payment to credit card payment."** *Robert Kiyosaki*

**Debit and Credit cards** have been a part of the banking landscape since the mid-1960s, so we can safely conclude that it is quite likely that our current customers and even their grandparents have used cards before. In other words, in the most likely scenario, the total number of Credit/Debit card users in your bank's database is higher than the total number of Digital Banking users. The gap between the two shows the potential you have for digital channels migration. Considering that a majority (if not all) of your customers are familiar with the card world (physical card and card's PINs), then why don't we utilize this familiarity factor to increase migration to digital channels?

When we look to the market, there are two common ways of using Credit/Debit Cards as an access tool to Digital Banking: CARD LOGIN and ONLINE BANKING APPLICATION via the CARD. Ideally, you can have both and their contribution to your banking base would not be less than 50 % - by experience.

Let me explain in more detail...

**CARD LOGIN** means that you let your customers use your online (internet and mobile) banking service without enrollment. Once again, no application for Digital Banking access – anyone with a Debit or Credit Card can login to your online banking, anytime they want (they watched your ad, a friend told them about your services, or they can't sleep at night!) – Such a convenience isn't it? All that is needed is the card and PIN.

**How to facilitate this service? You ask your client to complete three fields:**

> Last four digits of their card (or any fields you want.)

> Client Number (or Citizenship Number, maybe GSM number.)

> Card PIN.

Then she/he is IN! You can optionally set an activation code via SMS to client's GSM number for the first set up – if you want to have some extra security. Also, you can decide which services will be available for Card Login: Full functions or Card Related transactions/services only. It is up to you!

**ONLINE BANKING APPLICATION via CARD** means you set up a web based password application flow, in which the card information and PIN are used to authenticate the client. By this way, the total number of information gathering fields and time required to complete application is minimize. That means successful conversion rates would be quite high.

In addition to Card Information, some unique identifier questions might be asked of the client too. Then they show the ID, (recall from previous tips – make the default ID something the client already knows!) let the client set up the password – DONE! This can be completed in less than a minute...

Almost all Turkish Banks, as international ones HSBC and ICICI have been utilizing Credit/Debit Cards for on boarding to Digital Channels. PCI DSS Regulations (the agreement between your bank and the card provider) should be carefully analyzed and the consensus should be set between the two parties – before you launch such a service.

Don't get me wrong, I do not mean that physical cards are the future or forever with us – such assumption would be ridiculous considering the magnificent change in this area. At the same time, they exist today and can be used in order to access the Digital Banking...for at least a few more years. (Hopefully this will give me enough time to update the tips and produce new ones!) Also, we should consider that the inevitable end of plastic will not necessarily mean the end of the credit/debit card business. I think one way or another banks will always need to authenticate clients - so the existing systems may transform into another form, possibly to phone or something wearable, even a chip.

Final words: there are nearly 10.000 card transactions around the world every second. Credit/Debit Cards & PINs are used every day by our clients so they don't need to push themselves to remember these credentials. It is a mistake to underestimate the number of clients who forget their Digital Banking USER IDs and PASSWORDs and then become inactive. Effective use of Credit/Debit Cards almost totally eliminates this problem!

IN A NUTSHELL

There are two common ways of using Credit/Debit Cards as an access tool to Digital Banking: Card Login and Online Banking Application via the Card. Ideally, you can have both!

## CHAPTER 4

**"Two wrongs don't make a right, but they make a good excuse."** *Thomas Szasz*

The total number of online banking users is one of the main Key Performance Indicators for tracking the performance of Digital Banking.

Ideally you will have strong growth annually, beat the competitor's (or overall market) growth and have more online banking penetration than your country's internet penetration. As we do not live in the ideal world, this is not the case for most of us. That is why we need to find creative ways (in a tight budget and resourceful use of time) to increase the total number of digital banking users. In this chapter, I will talk about one of these ways, and I hope you will find it applicable and useful. I presented this solution four years ago in Las Vegas at an Innovation Competition where it won a gold medal. It has been officially recognized and adapted in different parts of the world in recent years.

When you look at the total number of online banking users and compare it with the previous year or month, you will see a change, either negative or positive. Hopefully this change is positive (that is why you keep your job and choose to read books like this, right!?) Let's say you have 10,000 more clients compared to the previous year. Does that mean that you have won 10,000 clients? In total YES, but it could be that you might have won 100.000 new clients throughout the year, but 90.000 of them have left (or are lost) so you ended the year at 10,000. Churn is one of the biggest problems Digital Banking managers must deal with. Three to seven percent, sometimes even higher, churn rates can be observed in many bank's client base. Therefore, we need to do something about it - even if we cannot make the churn rate zero (that would be nice), we can reduce the churn rate to help accelerate our client base's increase.

There could be many reasons for churn. One of them is very simple. a blocked password. If a client is locked out of their account and they have to call to get a new password - they stop using online banking. For this reason, clients will often need some encouragement to get a new password. I have an excellent solution to this problem, but you will need a couple of components first: A Fraud Detection System, CRM, Predictive Dialer, Online Password Application and a Call Center Agent. If you have them all, let us go a little bit further...

Fraud Detection Systems (FDS) monitor online banking client's activity, 24/7. A blocked password is one of the suspicious activities FDS observes. So if any password is blocked, FDS sees and knows (by comparing the profile information of client) whether the blocking action comes from a real client or not. If FDS concludes that the blocking action is done by the legitimate client, then it contacts with the CRM (Customer Relationship Management) system about the client's number. Now, with CRM at work, it checks the status of the client (mass, affluent or private.) Depending on the rule set it operates in - CRM contacts with the Predictive Dialer at the Contact Center to call the client. Then the magic happens! Within a few seconds following the blocked password, the client's phone (together with the agent's) starts ringing!! Then a call center agent helps the client reset their password by assisting him/her via online password application.

This surprise call, made more than 50.000 times per year, ensures that clients are happy and helps them to continue to use the service. You might try this simple, straightforward solution. From Asia to US, many colleagues of mine have implemented this solution and have had quite a number of positive results.

Understanding the reasons for Churn and Inactivation is the first step in addressing the problem. As I said, a blocked password is one of them, but there are many others too. If the client has become a dormant client and has stopped all banking activity, there is not much you can do to activate him/her – do not waste your time and energy over there. Just focus on the clients who are active in your bank, but inactive in Digital Channels. Also the time of inactivation is an important detail. It is relatively easy to win back recently churned clients than long term inactive clients. Monitoring client activities, even going further and estimating the likelihood of being churned, will give you some buffer time to address the problem.

Setting up a game plan against Churn and Inactivation helps to improve your chance of winning back your clients. You should work on some scenarios and ask yourself questions like:

1. What happens if a client forgets or blocks his user ID/Password? How will they get a new one or what kind of automated actions are taken by your bank to encourage the client to ask for a new password?

2. Do you regularly monitor and report the total number of clients who become inactive and analyze the reasons for their inactivity?

3. Is there a regular/ongoing campaign or promotional activities for Inactive or Churned Clients? If so who is managing it? Is it centrally or locally coordinated? Is there any budget allocated for this purpose?

4. Are regular actions are taken for dormant Digital Banking clients? If so what are they? Are there any automated or manual set of actions to prevent churn (or maintain retention)?

As you might guess, losing clients is part of the Digital Banking game. However, the amount and ratio of that loss is the differentiator between winning and losing the game. Getting new clients is always harder than keeping the ones in hand. If you can read the churn signals given by the unsatisfied clients – then you have a much stronger chance of winning them back.

### IN A NUTSHELL

Understanding the reasons for Churn and Inactivation is the first step in addressing the problem. If the client has become a dormant client and has stopped all banking activity, there is not much you can do to activate him/her – do not waste your time and energy over there.

## CHAPTER 5

**"Get your facts first, then you can distort them as you please." Mark Twain**

Knowing how your Digital Channels are performing is very important, as we cannot MANAGE something, we cannot MEASURE. (Tiger Woods once tried this and wanted to manage an extra marital affair without measuring the numbers and the poor guy within a year, agreed to a $750 million divorce!) Therefore, we need to have solid KPI's for monitoring Digital Channels contributions to our daily business.

As of today, there is no common standard for Digital Channels Metrics (i.e. KPI's or Key Performance Indicators). From one bank to another, KPI's are changing and if not set up right, they can be misleading. In order to know where we are (AS IS) and where we want to go (TO BE) – it is obvious that we need solid Digital metrics through which we can evaluate the performance of our channels on a routine basis.

**Traditionally there have been three main expectations from Digital Channels:**

> **REDUCING COST:** Transaction Migration from high cost channels to the low cost ones, ideally to Internet and Mobile.

> **REVENUE GENERATION:** Fees, Commissions and Sales from Digital Channels.

> **CLIENT SATISFACTION INCREASE**: Empowering the clients and supporting them through self-service channels.

According to these expectations, the very first KPI produced and very commonly used has been "The Total Number of Clients login to the internet or mobile banking" (the in the last 90 days as the standard). So it is assumed that the more clients using your digital banking, the more successful it is. This is partially true but not completely. This KPI alone provides a tunnel vision as not all logins mean a transaction that is required to capture the value from Digital Channels. So we need to have more KPI's in order to understand 360 degrees of the Digital Channel's Performance.

# Tolga Tavlas

## Here are the top 18 Key Performance Indicators / Metrics for Digital Banking:

1. **Customer Numbers:** Client logins, Clients performing financial transactions, inquiry only users, unique client logins per day, churn rates, inactive customers, blocked passwords, etc.

2. **Transaction Numbers and Volumes:** Total number of transactions and their share in bank, volumes of the transactions, penetration of specific transactions, channels only products performance, etc.

3. **Segment Penetrations:** Customer Segment based penetration of Digital Banking Channels (x % of mass clients, y% of private clients)

4. **Product Sales:** Total number of products sold online or leads created to the other channels.

5. **Fees and Commissions:** The revenue produced by Digital Banking channels in the form of transaction fees (like money transfers) and/or commissions (like stock trade.)

6. **Customer Satisfaction Index:** Measuring how happy clients are with the service they get, using internal or external client satisfaction surveys.

7. **Profit per client:** Totaling all revenues generated from Digital Channels and divide it by the total number of DB clients - so that finding how profitable a DB client is. (This would be very useful when you prepare business cases for new projects and products.)

8. **Cost per Transaction:** Totaling all ongoing costs (HR, servers, licenses, fees, etc.) created by Digital Channels and divide it by the total number of DB transactions - so that finding out the cost per transaction.

9. **Conversion Rates (Sales and Lead):** Total number of clients starting sales/lead process, versus the ones who successfully finish.

10. **Abandonment Rates:** Total number of clients who started an application via Web site, but not completed or abandoned the process. The reason could be a technical error or complicated steps. In order to increase the effectiveness of online sales capability – it is very important to know the reason(s) and solve the problems in the flows as early as possible.

11. **Service Interruptions:** How frequently have you experienced a Service Interruption and how much business have you lost in a given time period?

12. **Cross / Up Sales Rates:** Selling more

than the product itself – in the form of offering related or more profitable products is an excellent way of generating extra revenues. If you closely monitor how you perform this art, and fine tune your processes to make it happen – success is easy to reach.

13. **Problems Reported / Customer Support / Complaints:** Number of reported incidents, Most frequently experienced problems, total number of support calls and complaints from your call center or social media accounts.

14. **User Experience:** It is about listening and reporting the overall conversation about your bank, through social media – mobile application markets or any other online community areas where your bank's reputation exists.

15. **Frauds:** Number of incidents, losses if any or blocked fraud attempts, types and methods of attacks, performance of monitoring tools, etc.

16. **Market Share:** How is the overall digital market performing against your performance and what is your market share?

17. **Country          Online/Mobile Penetration:** Total number of people online in your area or total number of

smart phone owners versus – your digital banking penetration in your client base.

18. **Branch Support Measurement:** Highest and lowest performing branches to support (in the form of on boarding) Digital banking channels, total number of passwords distributed via branches, etc.

These are commonly used KPI's in order to measure the performance of Digital Banking performance, but of course there could be many more. (Please feel free to share - if you know any other useful ones).

Ideally, Digital Banking Index information should be accessible in real time and filtered by time (like a year, month, week or day). In this way you can see how your Digital Channels are performing and what kind of corrective actions are required, if needed.

IN A NUTSHELL

We cannot manage something, we cannot measure. Traditionally there have been three main expectations from Digital Channels:

> Reducing cost

> Revenue generation

> Client satisfaction increase

**"We owe a lot to Thomas Edison - if it wasn't for him, we'd be watching television by candlelight."**
**Milton Berle**

"Video Banking" has been a hot topic in the Digital Banking area for some time. Both Fintech companies and banks are so interested in this technology to facilitate banking services above the pre-defined limits in the banking perimeter. It is usually positioned as the substitute to Face to Face banking. There are many banking services provided via Video Banking from Customer Onboarding, to Money Transfers. Not very widely used yet, but some say it is the future of banking!

**What is it?**

Video Banking (VB), also called remote banking, may be defined as providing assisted banking services to clients via video connection. Considering banks have many channels to provide remote service to their customers, what makes Video Banking unique for clients is interacting with the bank staff via video connection, face to face, for a customized service. This unique feature could be very useful in complex banking procedures, like first time account opening or buying a complicated bank product or service.

Customers can use Video Banking via Video Teller Machines, video kiosks, Smartphones / tablets or PCs. Video-teller machines (distant cousin of traditional ATMs) and Technology Branches (by the way, is there any bank branch without this technology!) are the typical forms of Video Banking used in bank perimeters. As the connection speed inside the bank perimeter is higher than residential or on air connections, the performance of VB is much better at in-house applications.

**The main advantages:**

Video Banking provides a huge convenience for banking interactions. There is no time or location limitation, it can be done from a bank branch or client's home. Wherever the camera, connection and voice are available – VB can be used. As current mobile devices have all the prerequisites needed for Video Banking, it is safe to assume that any client with a Smartphone is ready for Video Banking. Anyone who can use Skype can use Video Banking services too.

Another advantage VB bring to the table is an increase in transparency and trust for both sides: the clients and the bank. Clients feel much more comfortable when they see a representative and get assistance when they need it. For the bank's side, seeing the client helps to prevent identity theft and reduce fraud risks. Furthermore, Video Banking may give your bank an opportunity to reach clients that are out of your branch network coverage. This point might become very critical, if the branch closure is in your agenda – that has been experienced by many banks in the western world.

Enriching User Journey with Video can create positive effects about the perception of banking services, too. It could be used for support or selling processes, to increase the effectiveness of the practice. Although we are all going digital, there is still a need and demand for humanizing the processes. As banking has been moving from transactional to relational practices, video banking could be a useful tool to facilitate relationship building between the bank and the clients.

New generations of clients give so much importance to financial advice, therefore providing such service via video banking would be very welcomed. Also, traditional banking hours does not often fit with the banking needs of the Digital Clients who may need such assistance at any time of the day. This may also create some positive results like reducing branch traffic and contribute to your branch migration efforts.

Also you might observe that there has been a great change in regulations in the financial area. KYC (knowing your client) is more important than ever, this is very critical to prevent online frauds. Account Opening processes should be monitored and observed carefully and identity verification with only text or voice may not be enough to meet the high standard of new security checks. That is where Video Banking might come to help too.

**How common:**

As of today, it is not possible to say that Video Banking has been used widely, but it has a strong potential. There are many banks all over the world that have been trying to do something innovative and useful with Video Banking. There is no winning formula yet, but everyone agrees on the idea that in the future, remote banking will be a critical part of daily banking practices.

There are also some limitations on Video Banking too, as it heavily depends on connection speed – if the required infrastructure is not in place – rather than creating a positive impact, VB may be source of a huge frustration on the client's side. Moreover, it is critical to note that it should be used to simplify the user experience – not vice versa. Providing such service does not guarantee the adaptability on the client's side and this is one of the side effects observed by many pioneers of this service.

Typical Video Banking practices you can observe in the banking area are: Mortgage Advisers, Digital Onboarding Specialists, Insurance Sellers and High-net worth portfolio advisors. Why? Because providing VB service is not inexpensive. So you need to analyze the target segment for such a service very carefully. Especially if the main focus is to set up and maintain a strong relationship with the client, you better go for Private and Affluent ones. By this way your upsells and X-sells justify the cost.

Accordingly, there is also a need for product and service selection, not every product is profitable enough to sell or serve through video banking channels. I should also note that there is a need for solid training for the bank staff involved in the party!

IN A NUTSHELL

Video Banking provides a huge convenience for banking interactions. There is no time or location limitation, it can be done from a bank branch or client's home. Wherever the camera, connection and voice available – VB can be used.

# GENERATING REVENUE

## CHAPTER 7

**"Marketing is a contest for people's attention."** *Seth Godin*

Digitalization transformed customer behaviors and their expectations from banking; this forces us to change the way we do marketing. As a result of this transformation, customer's decision journeys have been altered radically and financial services are under heavy pressure to adapt to this. At present, "Cross channel," "targeted" and "just in time" offers are required to attract the attention of digital customers both at online and offline platforms. As the role is defined for Digital Channels upgraded from Transaction Migration to Revenue Generation, these channels can help the bank while moving into the "all marketing must be digital marketing" era for success in the new economy.

Marketing our bank's products or services using digital technologies could be the simplest definition of Digital Marketing. Although the definition is quite simple, the impact it would create on banking is quite large. It necessitates digitalizing processes and the management of every single step of Customer Decision Journeys. Smart Decision making actions supported by a strong CRM integration would be the key that unlocks the potential of the new opportunities.

Defining digital customer experience is a very important first step. There is a need for leveraging customer interactions coming from different banking channels for the purpose of increasing customer engagement. So the banks are in a position of knowing the customer's next action is a basic survival need. Advanced Digital Analytics (which was mentioned in previous tips) is an asset that banks should have to set up some new engagement strategies related to customers' behaviors. The main factor of how we differentiate ourselves from the others will be how we engage our customers in our Digital Marketing activities.

In order to have a consistent digital marketing framework with both Online and Offline Channels, banks must offer "always-on" marketing programs. This is the new normal. Without Seamless and Engaging experiences provided by the bank to its clients, diminishing returns and poor audience engagement would be inevitable. The question we should ask ourselves is: "How can we provide the most value to our clients?" Answering this question will tell us what is needed to create a success story in Digital Marketing.

A solid Strategic Marketing & Sales Strategy for Digital should be our starting point. A "non-stop" marketing engine can be used for the "Next Best Action Predictions" of our clients. So we should be in a position to estimate and recommend what would be the customer's right next best action. This could only be possible if the customer's decision journey is understood well and all interactions are carefully customized. That should be our ultimate goal ...

What are the prerequisites of Digital Marketing and which tools should we have in our inventory?

We already know that the newest generation of clients are more likely to use their mobile devices as their primary mode of interaction. So there is a need for Responsive Designs regardless of the channels used to provide a seamless experience to the client, and Digital Analytics will be our key to set up the stage for establishing such a service.

Perhaps we may even need to go further and APP'ify the products/services in our perimeter in order to adapt the digitalization. Also the shift from Multi-channel (all channels sing the same song in different ways) to Omni-channel (all channels sing the same song in the same way and if one stops – another can continue where the first left off) is part of providing a seamless experience too.

## The twenty important components of Digital Marketing are:

1. Email and Video Marketing tools

2. Search Engine Optimization (SEO) for both paid and organic search

3. Having Earned Channels vs Paid Advertisement Channels

4. Mobile Marketing

5. Content Marketing

6. Marketing Automation

7. Digital Analytics (web, mobile, social and location based)

8. Optimized Landing Pages with Responsive Design

9. Getting regular customer feedback (Customer Listening)

10. Launching new products together with customers (co-product development)

11. Real Time CRM Integration with All Channels

12. Strong Reporting Features

13. User Experience Design

14. Digital Influence Management

15. Clear Call to Actions

16. Well Designed Marketing Funnel (pre-sales, sales, after-sales)

17. Clear set of roles and responsibilities for each channel

18. Product Blue Prints and Mapping (which product should be sold, where and how)

19. Driving Traffic with Fresh Content

20. Optimized Conversion Processes

If the components listed above can come together with the actions listed below – you can create a magical Digital Marketing success formula:

> **Using Contextual Selling Rules:** (that means we can sell our online products at the time of need. For example, selling travel insurance to clients who are in a different location or selling loans to clients whose account balance is lower than standing orders waiting.)

> **Displaying recommendations:** (almost every client loves reasonable advice. Look at Amazon's "those who bought this also bought this" approach. But you better be careful in this business to advise the products good for the bank and client – together. Not only one or the other. You know what I mean! Losing trust means losing business.)

➤ **Utilizing more mobile banking:** (everyone goes mobile and mobile tells a lot about what is going on in the client's life. If you need to bet on only one channel, it should be mobile. Even among the PC lovers, it is not a very common practice to take a PC everywhere with you – right?)

➤ **Having A Social media strategy:** (which we mentioned in other tips – please have a look at this.)

➤ **Customizing Content for every channel:** (if you tell a story in 100 words in the branch, it should be done in 50 at the ATM, 25 at Contact Center, 10 online and 5 on mobile devices.)

➤ **Performing Search Analysis:** (you need to analyze both internal and external search engine findings, which tells a lot about everything. For example, Google "genius" and count how many Albert Einstein pictures you get.

➤ **Creating Best performance tactics score cards:** (learn from experience. Find the best methods and repeat it.)

➤ **Setting up Event triggers:** (what should happen if X happens or what will follow Y.)

➤ **Shifting the budget from traditional channels to digital channels:** (if the clients surf more on the net, how come TV ads get a bigger budget than online marketing?)

## Tolga Tavlas

Before finalizing this tip, I would like to note that Digital Marketing cannot be a task executed by the marketing team only. IT, Corporate Communications/Branding, Channel Management and Branch Network Management teams need to be invited to the party too. Moreover, it is valuable to note that according to some researches, bank website conversion rate standards are around 10%, this is much higher than the other industries. If we can manage this potential well, Digital Banking can become the most profitable channel of the bank for sure.

IN A NUTSHELL

A solid Strategic Marketing & Sales Strategy for Digital should be our starting point. A "non-stop" marketing engine can be used for the "Next Best Action Predictions" of our clients.

## CHAPTER 8

## TIP EIGHT: WEBSITE MANAGEMENT

**"Web users ultimately want to get at data quickly and easily. They don't care as much about attractive sites and pretty design."**
*Tim Berners-Lee*

One of the most important digital assets a bank can have is their Website, maybe the most important of all. It is the bank's digital main gate from where our customers come to know about the bank's products and services, perform transactions via online banking or make purchase of financial products. The difference between a good website and a bad one could have a huge impact on the bank's online business. If the management of bank website is not done properly, then there will be a damaging gap between the customer's expectations and what the bank's digital deliverables are.

For the purpose of conveying the right message, I would like to differentiate between the bank's website, which everyone visits, and the bank's online banking service; also underlining the fact that the focus of this message is the website. In my opinion, a significant number of bank websites are performing below their potential and not managed well by the non-digital mind-set. This may result in some challenges like low conversion rates, narrow sales funnels and worst of all "not knowing what is going on the web." Actually it is not a hard task, it just requires some planning and execution.

First of all, we should have a business plan. I do not necessarily mean to create a new site (if you want to you can of course!). The operation area is our current website that has been live for some time (maybe 20 years but changed and transformed many times.) We need a web management plan and this plan should address three basic questions:

1. Who are the visitors and what is the purpose of their visit?

2. Which pages are visited most often?

3. What are we going to sell or promote?

The number of questions can be raised to hundreds but if these three basic questions are answered correctly, then you have a strong business plan in hand and you just need to stick to it. Let's go a little deeper with these questions and start with the first one.

# Tolga Tavlas

## Who are the visitors and what is the purpose of their visit?

There are two main categories of your visitors: **Your bank's clients** and **Surfing (non-bank) visitors**. If it is your bank's clients, there is segmentation: **digital banking clients** (they are authenticated, but most of the time they do not stay long on the web site, they go almost directly to the online banking service.) and **non-digital (yet) clients**. After this very high level of segmentation, it is easy to conclude that we should convert: Surfing (non-bank) Visitors to our customers (if available via online KYC or via branch KYC), our non-digital (yet) clients to digital banking clients, and sell our online products/services to our digital banking clients. Easy as pie, right?

How about the purpose of their visit? Maybe, to spend a longer time on our website. By reading annual reports, or playing with financial calculators? Perhaps just killing time as they have nothing else to do? Or the best of all, our sexy website design is so good that it attracts many visitors from all over the world just to see it! Well, if we do not know the reason of their visit, all assumptions above could be valid, but if you know the reason for the visit, then these assumptions are ridiculous.

As far as I have observed, people visit bank sites for three main reasons from pre-sales, sales and after-sales angles:

1. Interested in Bank Products and would like to know more about them.

2. Purchase a bank product (personal loan maybe) or to use a service (like online banking.)

3. Getting after sales support (branch locations, call center number, product details, complaints etc.)

Knowing the motivation for the visit can be the first step in providing a seamless customer service experience.

## Which pages are visited most often?

You can assume (don't do that or don't know that anyone else does) or you can use some analytical tools to see the "hot" pages on your website. This task is more than just seeing the numbers, rather re-visit your plans according to these numbers. Let's imagine your bank website has around 2.000 – 5.000 web pages. Do you know how many of them are hot, Maybe 10 or 20 (I call it "**The Critical 1 %** " – **Pareto rule for bank web site 1/99!**)  Which means you better make your hat tricks in these pages because the rest have no use for your critical actions.

(Just as in the real estate market, location, location, location is valid for websites too!)

The Critical 1% is the area where you should put your money and resources. It should have dynamic content, so your CMS (content management system) can take care of this. Also we cannot expect that every part of a critical 1% web page is equally visible to the visitors. In order to find out the most visible parts you may use eye tracking software too. Also if you have any chance use A/B testing, even if you do not have the software - it is not complicated: you may use one web page template a week (A), another template for the second week – see the difference between them and go for the on with a higher C2A (call to action) performance!

## What are we going to sell or promote?

Selling on the web is very different from selling in the physical world; it took time for some to get this. I personally experienced and saw that some product owners insisted on placing soft copies of the product application form online (and did it, and then blamed the web for low conversions! Ignorance is bliss, isn't it?) I am afraid it is not possible to sell every product we wish to sell online. For this reason, the products (loans, mortgage, insurance, credit cards, etc.) should be chosen carefully and crafted for digital sales. Some products are easy to sell (simple), some are not (complex). Not only products, but also services could be sold online too. Ideally, the sales process starts and finishes on the web – if not it should lead to the Contact Center or the Branch.

The best approach to Web based sales is to create product journeys for each selected product to be sold online. In this journey, all pre-sales, sales and after-sales activities, roles and responsibilities should be planned carefully. Then the sales funnels are monitored and adjustments are made if required.

Also, Positive Feedback about your website experience in Social Media works like a charm. You may have heard the term of PROSUMER – who could be your volunteers and help you to design bank products together. Keyword selection and SEO (search engine optimizations, Meta tags), Web Analytic Tools, and Customer Experience Management Suites are important parts of web management, which I will explain in more detail in upcoming tips.

People visit bank sites for three main reasons:

> ➢ Interested in Bank Products

> ➢ Purchase a bank product

> ➢ Getting after sales support

Knowing the motivation for the visit can be the first step in providing a seamless customer service experience.

## CHAPTER 9

"You can't just ask customers what they want and then try to give that to them. By the time you get it built, they'll want something new." *Steve Jobs*

The term, "Mobile Payments" may trigger different images in everyone's mind: from Apple Pay to paying parking fee via SMS. Although some players fight for the market dominance, it is hard to guess which one is going to win at the end – if there would be an end. Another interesting thing about Mobile Payments is its potential of being one of the biggest banking disruptions. In other words, it is an area in which non-banking player's direct involvement to the banking industry took place to eat some portions (if not all) of the "payment cake" of banking. So it might be worth our time to deeply analyse the topic a little bit more and see what is in it for us.

The terminology used for Mobile Payments (MP) is quite large and it may also be described as: "mobile wallet, mobile money or P2P" – unlike the terminology, what everyone has agreed on is the definition: "instead of paying cash or by credit card, customers pay with their mobile phones." So technically, anything you pay using your mobile phone is considered a mobile payment. Of course, there is an account or credit card registration required at the back end for funding.

Mobile Payments have been a growing business and has created a huge success story so far in different parts of the world. Most well-known examples are in Africa, where it was used to deliver banking services to an un-banked population. *(Whenever you feel pessimistic about where to find new clients, please consider that, according to many respected economic reports, 50% of the world is still un-banked!)* Apple Pay is another very successful model of Mobile Payments, which serves totally different segments with totally different business models. So there is no one success formula, rather some successful models are serving different needs, in different ways, in different parts of the world. It is up to you to find the correct formula in light of the market conditions your bank has been operating in.

**There are five common Mobile Payments models:**

    1. SMS – the payment transaction is done

via SMS, also called Premium SMS.

2. Contactless - NFC technology used and proximity required.

3. Mobile Billing – Payment is reflected in your bill by the service provider company.

4. P2P – One person sends money to another in a closed system via an App or Message.

5. Web Based - either via mobile app or browser, QR codes might be used too.

Your bank may provide all or some of the mobile payment options to your clients. One thing very critical to be kept in mind is, mobile payments itself is not something the client is interested in – rather client is interested in doing something else and MB should be positioned to support the clients to achieve his/her goal. (For example, the *client would like to get a hot strong coffee in the morning, but does not like to carry cash or change*!) So from a Machiavellian perspective, the goal justifies the means used to achieve it!

As of today, Apple Pay is one of the most successful mobile payments developed and commonly used so far but not the only one. (*It should also be mentioned that being part of the Apple ecosystem is a bit expensive for many people but this does not change the fact that most of the revenue is generated there of course.)* There are others in the market too, including PayPal, Starbucks, Square and Google Wallet. As you probably know, anyone who purchased an app from Google Play or iTunes has already registered his/her credit card with the provider. So any app purchase is also a mobile payment too. Also, all Uber Payments are done using in app stored payment information. So mobile payment is everywhere we look!

One other interesting point is Wearables connection with Mobile payments. We may expect that wearables will give a new momentum to mobile payments and may re-define the Mobile Payments business. Not only MP connection, but also Data Collection and Predictive Analysis are the other benefits wearables will bring to the market (*probably that is why Apple Watch and Apple Pay were introduced on the same day by Tim Cook!*) As of today, it is hard to say that Mobile Payments or Wearables are in a mature position rather than a stage where mistakes are made and we learn from them.

You probably asked yourself, like I do: "What should be done to be part of the growing business of mobile payments and how can we position our bank in this game?"

"Should we stand by and wait or take a more pro-active position?"

## Tolga Tavlas

The heavy investors of Mobile Payments are GSM companies, Retailers, Payment Providers, Card Companies, Money transfer Operators and Technology Companies. Banks are not... Why? You know why, because we are happy with things the way they are. The unfortunate fact is now we have to compete with some new players that are not banks. (*It is like a NCAA team against NBA team, but the game is still basketball!*). Banks are usually in the back seat but we still have a good chance to win if we play our cards right.

First a solid Mobile Payments strategy is required. New business models and partnerships will help drive adoption and usage for sure, that is why they should be part of our MP strategy. Furthermore, as a part of this strategy you may take all or some of the actions below:

➢ Offer Mobile Money Accounts to your clients.

➢ Invest in Wearables - like Apple Watch.

➢ Position Mobile Payments as part of your Big Data management plans.

➢ Usually clients registered one or more than one card, so we better encourage clients to use our card with promotions and discounts in popular mobile apps.

➢ Integrate your Mobile Banking with Mobile Wallet solutions.

> ➤ Solve Security and Privacy issues to encourage the clients.

> ➤ Address Lack of NFC terminals to issue and consider them in your POS expansion plans.

In The future, I do not expect that one single Mobile Payment solution will be dominating the market – rather clients will use more than one solution depending on the context. And most probably, there would be more than one app in different devices – that is not necessarily only mobile phones. Banks should not only consider retail clients, but also merchants in this landscape. It may take some extra time for regulations to catch the ball but they will. If security and privacy issues are handled well, the potential is excellent!

## IN A NUTSHELL

The heavy investors of Mobile Payments are GSM companies, Retailers, Payment Providers, Card Companies, Money transfer Operators and Technology Companies. Banks are not.

## CHAPTER 10

## TIP TEN: GSM OPERATOR PARTNERSHIPS

**"Perfect partners don't exist. Perfect conditions exist for a limited time in which partnerships express themselves best."**
*Wayne Rooney*

There is a huge potential between these two for mutually profitable partnerships: from security to marketing. The common point between banks and GSM Operators is the client, who has been using the services of both. (In technical terms, the client is the "primary key.")

It is obvious that there are different GSM Operators in different countries with different capabilities. At the same time, there are also many common tools and services too on the GSM Technology perimeter. The best thing is to organize a meeting with the GSM Operator representatives and ask what they can do for you. Also mostly likely, even if there is a dominant one, there are more than one GSM Operators in your country - so you need to talk with all of them. Who knows, competition might empower your hand too.

"X does it, how come you cannot" is pretty motivating stuff for many!

I am not referring to the fantastic projects, (that unfortunately just don't work in practice) such as: GSM-Bank partnered mobile wallets or installing your bank's mobile application into the ROM of the phones - which GSM Operators sell. The ones I refer to are more practical and working examples. Here are some of the capabilities that might be possible to get:

> **Security Perspective:** If your bank uses SMS (Short Message Service) for security purposes (in the form of sending a One Time Password or activation/verification), then you better know that the one who gets this message is your real client. SIM CARD copying or ID Theft (then getting a new Sim Card on behalf of the client) is a quite common attack used by some fraudsters. Technically it requires sim card change, sometimes it takes quite a long time for the client to realize the service interruption (the fastest fraud attempt I observed was 32 seconds - can you imagine what happens if it takes one hour for your client to realize what is going on?). The bank never knows this – the only one who immediately knows that is the GMS Operator. The Value Added service is: **"Blocking Sending Security related SMS to**

**recently changed SIM cards for N amount of time or bank's approval.**" The system works like a charm for the Turkish banks, if the SIM card has been changed - GSM Operators do not send secure SMS. The bank informs the client on screen and tells them why this happened and then the client needs to call the bank or use an ATM to unblock the restriction (so two factors are in use). So SIM CARD copying or ID Theft is a not a threat any more.

➢ **Collection Perspective:** Someone owes some money to your bank but you lost the contact, you want your money back - that's why the collection department is involved. However there is one little problem, the phone number in your database is not valid any more - who can help? Sure GSM Operators! In most of the civilized world, all citizens have unique numbers (you probably heard about the Big Brother thing!) which are usually called such names like: social security numbers, citizenship numbers or tax numbers etc. The best thing about these numbers is that you cannot change them as you wish - so they are always yours. The idea is simple, you ask the GSM operator to send collection **SMS to your client's Citizenship number rather than GSM number**. Yes, they can do that and there are many decent clients who forgot to pay and do not know they owe something to the bank. One SMS could be enough to inform them about the problem and trigger the repayment.

➤ **Marketing Perspective:** As you might guess, location based services play a key role here. GSM Operators do have the ability to track the movements of everyone, including your clients. Most probably you already positioned your Branch and ATM locations in Google maps or something similar. In other words you have the coordinates of your Branch and ATMs. So half of the job is already done, the other half is what would happen if your selected clients approach your perimeter? Maybe send a SMS and say "Wouldn't you like to pay your debt since you are so close to the branch?" (no just joking, this is too much guerrilla marketing!) Rather, you might say "Mr. X - we have a special offer for you, just go to our ATM and select this option." Or "we need to ask you to sign some papers if you have some time please visit our branch."

➤ **Data Analysis Perspective:** Unlikely, what is commonly believed at the majority of the banks have quite a primitive database structure. The clients are categorized according to their financial assets and descriptive items used to define them, like male - married - 62 - lives in London etc. Currently we need more than this; we need more behavioral data to customize our offers for the clients. If we use a very narrow perspective, we have no chance of knowing a mass client in our bank - might be a private banking client of our competitor. Who might help, sure GSM Operators. Think about where the client lives, where she/he goes, which one she/he uses and how much telephone bill she/he pays, using data so much (but not using our mobile app - wait a minute!) ?

For sure, what you can learn about clients, depends on consent of the clients too. Also, the possibilities are endless - I just pointed out some based on experience...

## IN A NUTSHELL

The common point between banks and GSM Operators is the client, who has been using the services of both. (In technical terms, the client is the "primary key.")

## CHAPTER 11

## TIP ELEVEN: DIGITAL ANALYTICS

**"It takes considerable knowledge just to realize the extent of your own ignorance."**
*Thomas Sowell*

Reducing costs to serve was the first motivation when banks started to invest in Digital Banking. The idea was simple: migrating the transactions from branches (high cost channel) to self-service channels (low cost channels: ATM's, Contact Center, Internet and Mobile). Transaction Migration models have been successfully deployed by many banks so far. Internet and Mobile (digital) banking have done the heavy lifting for non-cash transactions and proved their value to the banking industry. After the maturity was reached for Transaction Migration, the shift moved from Cost to Serve to Revenue Generation. Selling On-line is an important prerequisite for Revenue Generation and it requires having strong customer insight about what is going on your web, mobile and social perimeters. That is where Digital Analytics (DA) become involved.

Perhaps we should start with the definition. Digital Analytics (DA) is most commonly known as "Web Analytics" – this is understandable because it has started with it. However, according to current market standards, this is a very narrow definition because the scope is not limited with **web** only, but also **social** and **mobile (native & browser)** too.

Digital Analytic tools provide critical customer insight in four main categories:

1. **Traffic Stats** (page views, unique visitors, entry & exit pages etc.)

2. **Referrals** (where the visitors are coming from)

3. **Events** (what the visitors are doing – click through, downloads, error pages and other actions)

4. **Visitor Details** (browser, operating systems, etc.)

Yes, all advertisement materials by vendors can be summed up like this.

**Page Tagging** and **Server Log Analysis** are the two methods WA tools can gather client data. It is possible (and advisable) to use both of them together to get a better view of the client's online behavior. Depending on the tool you choose, customer data is stored **On Premise** (that means your bank's local servers) or **In-Cloud** (that means the tool provider's site). As bankers, we have strong tendencies to go with on premise solutions (we all know why!) but maybe it is time to trust the cloud a little bit more so that we can have better functionality at a fraction of the price.

Having digital customer insight means that you have an understanding of estimating and influencing the customer's behavior and convincing the clients to go for the call to actions (C2A). Digital Analytic tools can provide you this opportunity. Now, let's have a look at the topic from a banking perspective and ask ourselves: "What can Digital Analytic tools do for banking?" and "Which factors should we consider when you are choosing one or adding new functions to our existing tools?"

Although it changes from one bank to another, you can expect something around $5-7 dollars / month profit from a typical Digital Banking client's online (internet & mobile) banking activities. Broadly speaking, Digital Revenue Generation has three main sources:

1. **Fees** – derived from service charges or selected transactions like money transfers.

2. **Commissions** - coming from investment transactions like stock buy/sell, exchange and funds.

3. **Online Sales** - products, like loans – insurance and packages.

The best way to calculate such figures is to sum up the three source's revenues above, and divide by your active number of online banking clients. The First two are relatively easy to find out, but for the third one you need to reference your bank's overall profit table for the selected product. This is fine if you have end to end processes that means if the sales starts and finishes online. However, if your online sales process is not end to end, that means you create leads to other channels (maybe branch or contact centers) - either you need to use an application reference number, or you will have a very limited chance of knowing Digital Channel's contributions to the sales.

The big challenge for us, as the majority of the client's data is stored in a typical bank's database is descriptive. In other words, banks have a very narrow view of the clients, like: name John, male – lives in London – has house – is affluent, etc. Although Credit Card spending may give a better view regarding the client's position, it is still far from preparing the grounds for "moment of need" sales. However, if you have a well-designed online process *(it is important to note that in the internet world ugly - not well graphically designed - websites are usually the ones with the most money, like Google and Amazon!),* the way your client has been surfing through your bank's digital assets gives you critical clues about the client's needs. The keywords used, referrals, the time spent on the pages, banners clicked, calculations made, forms filled can tell you the story – if somehow all designed with the customer in mind and for a purpose: TO SELL.

Here's the top ten features you should look for when selecting a Digital Analytic tool:

1. CRM Integration

2. Customizable Dashboard (Analyzing data from multiple channels in a single interface.)

3. Real time customer path analysis.

4. Campaign Tracking with Campaign ROI measurement.

5. Retention, Funnel and Segmented Analytics.

6. User profiling with actions and goal tracking.

7. A/B Testing ability (which version of design or content sells the most?)

8. Strong Reporting (with charts and graphs.)

9. Heat Map Overlays (think an excel sheet with numbers and imagine that the highest figures are red and lowest ones

are green. Then assume that it's your web site's most seen or clicked sections!)

10. Voice of Customer ability (to get customer feedback about the experience, problems, etc.)

The main difference between selling on your bank's non-secure and secure zone is – client authentication. Anonymous surfers turn into bank clients once they log into the online (internet or mobile) banking. Some banks monitor client activities after clients are authenticated and waste valuable insight that could be gained from bank Website or Social Media perimeters of the bank. However, some of the Digital Analytic tools can store the anonymous surfing information and share with bank CRM as soon as clients have logged into the online banking system. This is an excellent opportunity to make a need based custom offer to the client – at the end of the day you know what she/he has been looking for, right?

If you want to sell online, Digital Analytics is not a "nice to have," it is a "must have" capability that should be in your landscape. Price may go from free to millions, but this does not guarantee the quality you will get. If you know what you think and how to use it, then even the most basic tool for DA can do the job!

## IN A NUTSHELL

Having digital customer insight means that you have an understanding of estimating and influencing the customer's behavior and convincing the clients to go for the call to actions (C2A).

## CHAPTER 12

## TIP TWELVE: MOBILE MARKETING

"The world is being re-shaped by the convergence of social, mobile, cloud, Big Data, community and other powerful forces. The combination of these technologies unlocks an incredible opportunity to connect everything together in a new way and is dramatically transforming the way we live and work."
**Marc Benioff**

Digital Transformation changed the way we live and do business, then gave two options to banks: CHANGE or DIE. As clearly stated by Darwin, neither the strongest nor the most intelligent, but the most responsive ones to change are the ones to survive. That is why many nice dinosaurs were dead, while not very advanced insects survived. (*You may consult to the cockroaches in your basement about their grandparents' success formula!*) Climate change was the change agent Darwin referred to, as of today the change agent is mobile. The way we respond to the mobile revolution will shape the future of the banking industry.

Much before the digitalization started, David Packard said that "**Marketing is too important to be left to the marketing department.**" If you have ever met (or worked) with any marketing professionals with limited understanding of the digital world, and observed the way they've used your (very valuable but limited) marketing budget – you might fully agree with him. It is a sad truth that banks are in the back seat of the mobile era compared to technology and telecom companies, which are looking forward to capture some of the market share from the banking business – unless the banks do something about this. Mastering Mobile Marketing is one of the most critical prerequisites to survive and foster in the new economy for the banking industry.

### What is Mobile Marketing?

The simple answer is marketing on your customer's Mobile Device. By definition, the mobile device is often a "smartphone," but not always. It could be simple phones, tablets, wearables (watch, glass), media players, handheld game consoles or even cameras. The unique feature of mobile marketing is providing an excellent opportunity to promote our services and products to our clients; anytime, anywhere and in a personalized way. The data coming from mobile devices may be turned into knowledge to influence or predict the next action of the client – via mobile marketing.

There is no single right way, but many interesting ways for Mobile Marketing. It can be accomplished through a variety of channels and forms, the popular ones are:

1. **SMS and MMS** (SMS is the most common but MMS gets more attention)

2. **Push Notifications** (via App or GSM Operator support)

3. **In App** (via downloaded native apps)

4. **QR Codes** (online and printed materials can be used)

5. **Mobile Web** (html 5 helps a lot on this)

6. **Bluetooth** (physical presence and device compatibility is required)

7. **Proximity** (the name tells the story right?! Ok may be not, how about ibeacon and NFC?)

8. **Location Based** (knowing where the client is will surely create very unique selling opportunities)

9. **Email** (is there anybody who does not read his/her emails from their mobile device?)

10. **M-Social** (Majority of the users use social media with Mobile Devices)

Mobile is not a platform on which we can push our marketing materials; it is also a platform that gathers client information, which we can use to prepare our marketing materials to produce better and more poignant offers.

According to some researchers, consumers use mobile devices more often, but in shorter periods of time, to research and buy products. Google named this trend as "**Micro moments**." What a fantastic definition, isn't it? We have only micro moments to deliver a strong marketing message and convince our clients to use the C2As (Call to Action) we've prepared for them.

There is a strong need for short, clear, persuasive and relevant content to succeed in mobile marketing. In order to prepare such content, we need **Mobile Analytics** too - as it helps us understand what our clients are doing with their mobile devices and when it is the right time (let's call it moment of need!) to offer a product / service to them.

There are some unique points that should be taken into consideration in terms of Mobile Marketing:

1. **Mobile App vs Mobile Web** differentiation is important. Providing a web based mobile banking service is much easier than providing native apps. However, native apps are much more capable of gathering data and producing offers.

2. **Apps Stores** are very critical places and the experience should be optimized. You cannot just upload your app and assume that your task has been done. Monitoring client feedback, answering questions – solving problems and changing your priorities in the light of client expectations is a must.

3. **Mobile device variety** is much more effective than PC variety, in terms of device capabilities - connection speeds, screens size etc. So before pushing a campaign all these variables should be taken into consideration, A/B tests should be done and responsive design principles should be employed.

4. **As the majority of clients read their emails on mobile**, Email marketing should be seen as part of mobile marketing and Email designs should be optimized for mobile screen sizes too. (*There is a false perception that assumes Email marketing is free, no it is not. Someone should be paid to design the mails and should design them well.*)

5. **Avoid Flash Ads** for mobile, this is a mistake many advertisers make (It's kind of a "if all you have is a hammer, everything looks like a nail" thing!).

6. **Only prepare clear, short, personalized content** and keep your audience in your mind. (The banking industry has a

reputation for "boring" – we do not need to sustain this image, at least for mobile. The biggest challenge I experienced while writing my book was not contributing to the boring banking literature!)

7. You've probably heard of **Mobile First Design**, which was first introduced by Luke Wroblewski in 2009 – who observed how much clients suffer while using small screens. The idea is to provide simple, adequate content for small screens and more features / content for bigger screens. It is also called progressive enhancement. Please make sure your landing pages are designed accordingly.

8. **Trying different tactics** and comparing their performance is essential for successful mobile campaign management. The goal is to collect behavioral data as much as possible to fine tune the offer.

Before finishing this tip, it is worthwhile to note that providing in store, branch or ATM free Wi-Fi access to get new clients or increase client loyalty is a very good idea. (if you ask them to tell you where they are, you will get a resounding NO, but if you provide free access - they will tell you where they are voluntarily.) We all know that buyer behavior leans toward mobile shopping, so help them shop – like Levis did for gold miners (*you remember this from the Location Based Services tip?!*), facilitate their need to access the net.

Also be quick, as Apple and Google have been working to develop technologies to block mobile ads!

IN A NUTSHELL

The unique feature of mobile marketing is providing an excellent opportunity to promote our services and products to our clients; anytime, anywhere and in a personalized way.

## CHAPTER 13

## TIP THIRTEEN: DIGITAL BANKING SECURITY

**"I am regularly asked what the average Internet user can do to ensure his security. My first answer is usually 'Nothing; you're screwed."** *Bruce Schneier*

One of the main challenges Digital Banking professionals face is to find the equilibrium point between security and functionality. At the end of the day we all want to provide the best digital banking experience in the most secure way. So is this possible? I think it is. I like the "functional security" expression, which means security enabling the business, rather than disabling.

When I started my career as an internet security professional back in 1998, before we started to work on an online banking project, the very first task given by the bank to me was to monitor erotic website visiting employees! For the last 17 years, I have not met a single "porn site visiting bank employee.," which tells me that some risks are real, and some are not.

If the balance between security and functionality is not set well, security can become a huge obstacle in front of Digital Banking channels. Client engagement, and keeping them active is the main target of digital bankers. If your security structure does not make things easier on your side, at that point you should reconsider what kind of improvements are required.

On the other hand, if your digital banking perimeter is not secure enough: you may end up with a loss of reputation, money and business. Security is a journey, not a destination. In other words, you will always need to do something about it – like updating yourself, your tools and technologies against constantly changing threats and the cybercrime landscape. And whatever you have in your perimeter – they should work together, like a football team (preferably a German football team, they always play the finals at the world cup – regardless of the generation!)

So what do you need to prepare a nice security cocktail for your bank?

1. Client Awareness.

2. The Right Staff skills (branch and head office) with a security mind-set.

3.  Personalized Security Settings for all Digital Channels.

4.  Offline Security measures supporting online security.

5.  Two or Three factor authentication tools (u know, u have, u are)

6.  Fraud Detection System – that monitors blocks and reports suspicious client behaviors.

7.  Real Time Alerts (both for clients and fraud team.)

8.  Cooperation with 3rd party (GSM Operators, Infected PC checking companies, domain monitors)

9.  Regular Security Checks and Penetration Attacks.

Yes, that's it.

There are three Security Stages from a banking perspective: PREVENTION – MONITORING and POST FRAUD. Ideally, the majority of frauds are prevented by providing security tools/technologies and increasing customer awareness. The ones which cannot be prevented, should be monitored and blocked. Unfortunately, sometimes it is not possible to block all fraud (banks used to have a reputation for hiding them but not anymore) attempts and some money losses happen – this is where Post Fraud Actions are required.

Here's a Security checklist. I hope it will be useful on your side:

## PREVENTION

1.  Are security devices currently used by your Digital Banking customers? (User Id, Passwords, OTP, PKI, Biometrics etc.)

2.  Are there extra layers of security in addition to devices? (Like special questions, challenge response tactics, additional security settings - transaction limits, access & account controls, etc.)

3.  Are there any recent security products purchased but not yet deployed? Likewise, what are the ongoing IT projects related with security? If so when will they deliver what?

4.  Are there any ongoing security activities like staff trainings or customer consciousness increases?

5.  Which mechanisms are used in order to track INSIDER supported fraud activities - was there any case experienced before?

6.  What is the level of cooperation between the bank and related security bodies (police, intelligence services etc.)?

7.  Do branches get regular security training? What is the level of security awareness

among branch staff (x over 10)?

8. Which tactics and tools are used to raise the level of customer security awareness - how do customers respond to that?

9. Do you regularly hire third party security professional parties to check the security levels of our WEBSITE, INTERNET BANKING and MOBILE APPs? Or any internal body - like audit or internal control has ever evaluated level of security of Digital Banking?

## MONITORING

1. Which attack methods were used to steal money from the customers? What are the typical attacks met and what was done for this? (SMS forwarding, man in the middle, virus or Trojan)

2. Do you have a Fraud Detection System? What capabilities does it have?

3. Which teams monitor fraud and report to whom? What's their organization and FTE number?

4. Do we use real time monitoring and second/third authentication in case of suspicious activities?

5. Which third party security firms are working with the bank, and are there any

ongoing talks with any company - if so what is it about?

6. Do we have a set of predefined procedures that are used and utilized in the moment any attack takes place? Like sending info to clients, shutting down some services, preventing some access, etc...

7. Is there any security hole or weakness known but not addressed (or closed) yet?

## POST FRAUD

1. What is the FRAUD LOSS experienced every month/year? Is it regularly tracked and reported?

2. What happens after a fraud event took place? How was this event handled? Which procedures were followed and what type of customer experience lived?

3. Is there any legislative PUSH available in your country? Who pays for the customer loss?

4. How many hackers were arrested by now? Is there any central body of security knowledge you use within the bank?

5. Are banks working together in your country to fight against online fraud?

In addition to this checklist, you also need

some hard earned experience too. For example, if all of a sudden some rich clients are targeted – you need to discover who is the lucky bank employee who looked at all victims' asset information in the bank database. Or if you heard about a phishing attack, you need to visit there to leave some fake User ID and Passwords – then wait for the visit to see the profile of the attacker. Then use this knowledge to block other victims' accounts. My favorite one is dumping the attacker's phishing side with thousands of fake IDs & passwords from different IP's & profiles – so that it is not easy to find the real ones!

As I already mentioned that security is not a destination – it is a journey. Also it is an expensive art too, banks should pay for it – smart ones pay in the form of investment in security technologies, others usually pay for fraud losses. However, increasing security cannot be an excuse to kill the Digital Banking – which will save the future of banking. If the tight security measures put you at a disadvantaged position against competition (against other banks or the new competitors who are not banks), it is more harmful than fraud losses. BALANCE is the thing we all need, in security – in life and in mind.

Final words coming from a former lawyer and president of Harvard University, Derek Bok who said, "If you think education is expensive, try ignorance" (Probably he got angry on high price critiques and talked emotionally!) Please never try ignorance when the subject is security!

## IN A NUTSHELL

If the balance between security and functionality is not set well, security can become a huge obstacle in front of Digital Banking channels.

## CHAPTER 14

**"It is a fraud to borrow what we are unable to pay."** *Publilius Syrus*

In the previous Digital Banking Security tip, I mentioned what is needed in order to prepare a nice security cocktail for your bank and Fraud Detection System (FDS) is one of the most critical components of it. FDS is the bottom of a full glass of water, if it is broken – the water (in our case money!) flows away. For this reason, it deserves a higher level of attention.

In simple definition, Fraud Detection System is software that monitors suspicious activities in Digital Banking and may produce alerts (even blocking the transaction) if the risk score is high. The risk score is calculated in light of the predefined variables (that are called rules) – like the money transfer to an account the first time, the amount of money or time of the transaction. As fraudsters regularly change tactics, FDS systems should be flexible enough to respond to these changes too. Also like a car needing a driver (sure driverless cars are on the way – literally and metaphorically! but still), FDS needs fraud specialists for management.

As banks deal with money, they also deal with all money related risks. Not only Digital Banking, but also Credit Cards – ATMs and Branches (including both internal and external) are subject to these risks. For this reason while some banks prefer enterprise wide - central solutions, others go with decentralized multi FDS's. Both approaches have advantages and disadvantages - that is why "one size fits all" is not working here. Fraud History and Potential Threats banks face should be the base of requirements analysis done for the bank. "I am not rich enough to buy cheap things" is a perfect explanation for FDS. Don't focus on the price as a main selection factor. The common practice I have observed is usually the bank pays what they need to pay, – sooner or later – from the right or left pocket.

The fuel of FDS is data, which is captured from the Digital Channels (or wherever FDS is supposed to protect). Data Mining and Data Analysis done by FDS to create a Risk Scoring Table and the results shared with the Fraud Detection Specialist. If the settings of the FDS are not done well, it might produce so many irrelevant alerts (called false positives) or it might not understand a real fraud case. None of these two options is desirable for the bank, in order to overcome this problem scenario based fraud detection templates and rule based actions used for FDS management. Plus, client profiling – that means recording how usually clients behave and detection when abnormalities happen (kind of a technical version of "you are not the man I married!")

You may prefer to develop your FDS in-house or you may go for a ready based solution, depending on your needs and resources. In either case, you need to check if it has:

1. Fast learning capability (would you like to wait six months for full profiling or would you prefer something that produces full profiling in a week by using the past six months data?)

2. Custom Fraud Parameters (rules, scenarios) with Immediate Update flexibility.

3. Knowledge base Share (if another bank already suffered from a type of attack, would you like to learn it the hard way or easy way?)

4. Both Internal and External Fraud Monitoring ability (sometimes fraudsters get some internal support) with real time Alert Mechanisms for clients and employees.

5. Fraud Pattern recognition and auto blocking / asking extra security approval features.

6. Easy to use Management Dashboard.

7. Strong reporting features.

In a typical Digital Banking Service, 10% or less of the transactions/services provided are risky and should be monitored by Fraud Detection System. However, this figure refers to the transaction/function set – not the transaction numbers. If we look at this from transaction numbers window, then money transfers and payments are the most frequently done transactions.

So which transactions should be monitored by Fraud Detection Systems? The list should include (but not limited to) the transactions listed below:

> Money transfers (Internal and External – but you can create some white lists so that you do not need to monitor the trusted records)

> Payments (Bank wire, services, utilities, standing orders, online purchases)

> Currency Exchange (by client or third party requests)

> Mobile Payments (p2p or proximity)

> Virtual Cards

> Top ups to Account (like prepaid cards,

or via debit/credit cards)

➢ Withdrawals from account

➢ Acceptance of Payments

➢ Contact Information Change

➢ Early Termination of Time Deposit Account or other investments

➢ Late night currency exchanges

➢ Credit Card Payments (once I saw a case in which both the client's credit card and digital banking credentials were stolen. The criminals were not able to transfer the money out of the account but tried to use the credit card payment option to increase the limit of the card they stole.)

Another interesting experience I think worthwhile to mention is, most of the Fraud Detection Systems do assume that family members do not steal from each other. I think the capabilities of an angry spouse or drug using child should not be underestimated. In technical terms, we may say that they do not rely only on profile based monitoring or past data, but program your FDS to track any kind of abnormality even between (so-called) trusted parties.

As final words, it is highly critical to note that even the best FDS in the world is not enough to handle the Fraud problem on its own. It is a strong security layer for sure, but there are other layers needed too (which I mentioned in – Digital Banking Security).

In addition, there is a need for specialized, intelligent and quick to learn groups of people to manage FDS. The partnership between banks against fraudsters helps to increase the chance of success too. I expect local banking authorities to encourage such partnerships

## IN A NUTSHELL

"I am not rich enough to buy cheap things" is a perfect explanation for FDS. Don't focus on the price as a main selection factor. The common practice I have observed is usually the bank pays what they need to pay, – sooner or later – from the right or left pocket.

## CHAPTER 15

## TIP FIFTEEN: HOW SMART PHONES ARE HACKED?

**"Nothing can bring a real sense of security into the home except true love."**
**Billy Graham**

Criminals always go where people go - this was the first thing we learned on the first day Criminology class. (Sure together with many other interesting things, but please note that there were no Discovery Channel's Crime documentaries available back in 1996!) Criminal mindset is quite simple and follows where the money goes. When it was asked "why do you rob the banks?" to one of the most charming and intelligent bank robbers, Willie Sutton (who had forty years of interesting criminal career), he answered "because that's where the money is." Yes, it is that simple...

As of today, we know that the future of banking will be mobile - so we can safely estimate that mobile will be the target for hackers. If you have a look at the security trends, you can easily see that the variations and types of attacks have a very strong direction to mobile platforms. The most heartbreaking fact is the ability of mobile apps developed by fraudsters (let's call them malware) are much better than the legitimate banking apps (shame on us!) In other words, they know more about our clients than us. The unfortunate result is, if you heavily rely on client profiling in your security perimeter - criminal activity will be very hard to detect.

According to my experience, Mobile Security is a sensitive topic. It is not about only providing services, but also the fact that using them affects us in our personal lives. Mobile Phones have been indispensable for many of us, with their amazing contributions to our lives. They are with us 24/7. They listen to what we talk about, come where we go, know our friends, take our pictures, recognize our music taste, access our Facebook Account, know our bank credentials, read our messages/emails and can do many more awesome activities – but how secure are they? How are we going to protect ourselves, our loved ones and our companies against the dangers of the mobile world?

Let's start with the common risks for mobile:

1. Viruses, worms , Trojans or other Mobile specific malware

2. Theft of sensitive data

3. Drive by downloads and Update Attacks

4. Exposure of critical information through wireless and Bluetooth sniffers

5. Loss, theft or damage of device

6. Use of them as proxy to establish a virtual connection to an internal network

7. Data loss / leakage due to the small footprint and portability

8. Fraud enabled by remote access or copying mass amounts of sensitive data

9. Spam causing disruption and driving up service costs if targeted toward mobile

10. Malformed Message Service (SMS & MMS) messages causing devices to crash

And of course... SOCIAL ENGINEERING!

A couple of months ago I prepared a presentation on Cyber Security and shared with a friend, Brett King (you know him! He is one of the great masterminds of the Digital Banking area), for his feedback. He found the first draft of the presentation a little bit pessimistic and advised me to be more pragmatic on the subject. He was concerned the message might be perceived as "don't use digital because it's not safe." This was not my intention of course. I just wanted to deliver a simple message that is "the future is digital and we should know that mobile will be the landscape for criminal activities as a result of this change." As Brett said to me "he is a fan of the 'immune system' analogy when it comes to cyber security." This is an excellent definition - so we should work on developing this immune system for Digital Banking. The first step is to understand "what happens if the mobile device of a bank customer is hacked?" (Houston we have a problem!) Then we can discuss how it is hacked and what we can do about it.

I can write hundreds of pages on mobile security (more than a business, it is a hobby on my side - I even lectured the topic in a university!) but I won't. Rather I will sum up the motivation of hackers to attack Smart Phones – at the end of the day this book is about Simple and Practical Tips, isn't it? There are five ways mobile devices can be exploited:

1. **Stealing Data:** (from banking credentials to IMEI numbers, maybe contact list or call logs. Oh please, do not forget pictures too!)

2. **Monitoring:** (recording your conversations and watching what you are doing, reading your SMSs or knowing your location. Scary right?

3. **Using it for Botnet activity:** (let me tell you in this example: a group of criminals stole your car to rob a bank – so your device was used for an illegal activity and you are the one who is responsible to prove that it is not you!)

4. **Financial Risks:** (maybe international or hot line calls, sending premium rate of SMS messages or forwarding your bank's one time password SMSs)

5. **Controlling your activities:** (posting on social media or accessing your company network and use your device as a bridge).

We can say that iPhone is more secure than Android, as it has been using unique and centrally controlled operating systems. Also, market controls have been stricter. However this does not mean it is risk free. We are living in a world, in which hackers claim they can steal fingerprints from pictures or control airplanes via Wi-Fi access provided on board.

I have a strong reputation of being an Android fan since the initial release in 2008. Unlike Apple, it was designed for mostly technical people – with the idea that such people know what they are playing with. Google market controls were not strict on the apps because the assumption was there that an auto-control mechanism among the users and if something went wrong it would be reported and fixed. In other words, security was given to the hands of the end users. (If you are a late comer to the market, you need to make some tricks to catch the leader – this is what Google did!) As of writing, Android has 79% market share, and older versions of it are vulnerable to some known exploits. And the worst part of the story, a majority of the end users are not aware of that. So this puts a huge responsibility on your shoulders as a Digital Banker – you should protect your clients.

Before I finish this Digital Banking TIP, I want to share one additional insight from another Digital Banking Mastermind, Chris Skinner. I had some security discussions with him some time ago and he mentioned this in his blog with an article called, "How to be secure in an insecure world." If the subject is mobile security, this is what we should focus on "security in an insecure world."

## IN A NUTSHELL

As of today, we know that the future of banking will be mobile - so we can safely assume that mobile will be the target for hackers.

## CHAPTER 16

## TIP SIXTEEN: IF A CUSTOMER'S PHONE IS HACKED

"The Internet has fashioned a new and complicated environment for an age-old dilemma that pits the demands of security against the desire for freedom."
Misha Glenny

As we have discussed in the previous Digital Banking Tip, "What happens if a mobile banking user's phone is hacked?" Now it is time to go a little deeper into the subject. Mobile security is a concern or should be a concern for everyone, not only digital bankers. Mobile devices have become our ID's, probably you have heard the famous expression "you are who you hang out with" and most of us hang out with our mobile devices a lot!

When the "security" term evolved, it trigged in the minds of many people an image of extremely intelligent criminals with extremely intelligent tactics - kind of like it is rocket science. Although there are some very intelligent fraudsters with very smart tactics, the most common type of attacks are pretty basic and preventable with some simple measures. Usually the weakest link is the users, but at the same time media attention is always on high profile attacks rather than daily (business as usual) ordinary common attacks. This creates a false impression that security is very complicated and impossible to manage. This is not true. At the same time, it is worth noting that security structures should have multiple layers - not just one. And there is no 100% security for anyone, including: The White House, FBI, Papa, Kim Jong-un or the Queen. What you can do is make your domain harder to attack so that you will not be chosen as a target by criminals and they will go after another one under normal conditions.

Let's go back to mobile security, once I read an article on "what happens to your mobile after it is lost or stolen?" an experiment done by a famous security software company. As a part of the experiment, one of the experimenters needed to leave a mobile device on a table in a café and go. This was not as easy as expected, as societal rules were at work and there were decent people in the café most of the time. They informed the experimenter by saying "hey mate, you forgot your phone!" (so technically it is not easy to lose a phone, as you would expect!) After many trials, finally the phone got "lost" and activities were monitored. The expectation was to observe some financial actions (some banking apps, and fake passwords on notes) in a few minutes that never happened. Rather social media accounts were accessed! So we can conclude that for a random criminal, the magazine side of the phone is much more important than the financial part. However, this is not the case for financially motivated attackers.

From the digital banking perspective, there are seven players in Mobile Security Landscape:

1.  Builders (phone manufacturers, operating system providers, developers)
2.  Informers (traditional and social media)
3.  Legal Enforcement (Legislation, Police)
4.  GSM Operators
5.  Banks
6.  Customers - also can be called Targets
7.  Criminals

We can say that all six players on the white side have some roles and responsibilities in mobile security and should work together, ideally. Is this the case today? I am afraid not. There is a huge gap between where we are and where we should be. And this is known and exploited by the dark siders.

There are a couple of methods used by Hackers (I hate using this word for criminals, at the time I was learning about the computers this was the greatest level we wanted to reach, but now it has a negative meaning.) In order to hack mobile devices. I can only give broad definitions here so that you can go into more detail if you want by using them as search engine keywords:

1. **Phishing:** (same version of web attack. The idea is not to control your device but to get your critical information. Mobile web is the platform, mobile browsers without address bar are easy targets)

2. **Code Injection:** (native apps, first legitimate app submitted to the market and installed - then code injected version is installed as an UPDATE. As customer trust is already there, it is easy to fool anyone)

3. **Malicious SMS and MMS:** (name says so, right?)

4. **App Store Attacks:** (controls are stricter now but there are still some leaks and average response time of market is around eight days.)

5. **Malwares / Trojans:** (SMS forwarders, key and screen loggers.)

6. **Intercepting:** valuable financial information With Near Fields Communication.

7. **Bluetooth and Wi-Fi Attacks:** (free wifis - usually are not free, do not use them for

financial transactions.)

The motivation is to either capture some info or to control your device, mostly both.

The end result is: your pictures, your contacts, recording some critical conversations, using your device as a part of bot net (like stealing a car to rob a bank), your connections (to fool them phishing: like sending your Facebook friends some messages "I am in trouble, send me some money") etc...

As the final words, please note that most of the mobile devices are infected when they are connected to infected PCs, not when they are on their own.

And a bit piece of advice from uncle Tolga to Jailbreak and Rooted device owners (i.e. adrenalin lovers): please do not play with such toys unless you truly know what you are doing!

Next tip will be about what we can do to secure our digital banking service...

IN A NUTSHELL

Although there are some very intelligent fraudsters with very smart tactics, the most common type of attacks are pretty basic and preventable with some simple measures.

## CHAPTER 17

## TIP SEVENTEEN: VOICE BIOMETRICS

"A lot of companies are clueless, because they spend most or all of their security budget on high-tech security, like fire walls and biometric authentication - which are important and needed - but then they don't train their people." *Kevin Mitnick*

Providing digital financial services requires high levels of security both on the client and bank side. At the same time, Digital Banking growth can only be achieved if the security and the functionality are mixed in an equal balance. Otherwise security might become a business disabler. For this reason, Authentication of clients in a secure and easy way has always been a critical topic for Digital Banking. It started with User ID and Static Passwords, then followed by OTP (one time passwords) and PKI (public key infrastructure), finally biometrics arrived on the scene. Among all the other biometric solutions, Voice Biometrics (VB) has a special advantage: Convenience! It works with every mobile device (smart. dumb, expensive and cheap) plus even with landlines. Plus minimum user participation is required. So it could be a solid alternative to static passwords.

Even if currently used very widely, static passwords and OTP's will have no future in the authentication business - almost everyone agrees that the future of authentication will be Biometrics: (something that the client is.) Biometrics Authentication methods include (but are not limited to): fingerprint, face recognition, retina & palm scan and voice print. There are also some challenges coming with Biometric authentication too, and two of them are quite serious: first if it is stolen you cannot change it (unless you have a medical operation, it involves a high cost just to change the password isn't it?) and the second is you need a device to facilitate the biometric check. The first issue was solved by not storing the biometric Id, rather using an algorithm to produce a hash value and store it in the device or in a central server. For the second, you can use your mobile device or an independent reader connected to your PC.

## What is Voice Biometrics?

In the simplest definition it is a technology that recognizes the person from their voice. It is also called Speaker Recognition. Although it sounds very similar, there is a difference between speaker recognition (who talks) and speech recognitions (what is said.) Human anatomy (mouth & throat shape & size) and learned behaviour patterns (speaking style) create different acoustic patterns and this is the basis of Voice Recognition.

Voice Biometrics works in real time and requires no special reader. On the client side, there is just one thing needed - a microphone. As all mobile phones and telephones have microphones, we may say that all clients are ready for Voice Biometrics. They do not need to have cutting edge smartphones, even with the phones invented in 1876 - it is possible to use VB.

## How Voice Biometrics works?

At the time of the enrolment the customer's voice is recorded and later compared with the voice used for authentication. So comparison between the enrolled voice and authenticated voice is done. In other words, voice matching is required for authentication.

VB can be used as **Text dependent** (clients need to repeat a script or a word) or **Text independent** (clients just speak.) For security reasons, it is also possible to re-record every conversation with different salt value (salt is a random string of data used to modify an encryption) so if it is stolen, it can be re-recorded without any problem. This is an advantage over other biometric authentication methods.

There are two types of VB: **Active** (customer should say a script, text or just talk) and **Passive** (VB works in the background silently). Two of them can be used together (advisable!) or separately. (*Some Voice Biometrics solutions provide an ability to compare the voices of fraudsters with the voice used for authentication. That means if any fraudster tries to fool the system, the pattern is recognized and the fraud management team is alerted.*) Active is better in terms of higher accuracy and clear verification. But enrolment is required or no fraudster comparison function is available. Passive could be considered if enrolment is not wanted, but it produces less accurate results than the Active.

Voice print samples of clients are stored either in a **centralized server** or **user end points**. Server Side (or centralized) storage application should be given priority and this has the largest coverage of clients.

The future of digital banking is mobile and it is very simple to get the voice print of the client via mobile app too.

What kind of security benefits can Digital Banking get from Voice Biometrics?

## Tolga Tavlas

Easy enrolment and easy to use.

1. No more static passwords or OTP devices, covers all client base.

2. It can be integrated with Fraud Detection Systems so that it could be positioned as fraud prevention tool.

3. Improves Contact Center processes and reduces the time for waiting on the queues.

4. Speech Recognition, text or conversation based recognition, known fraudster identification functionalities can be used.

5. Provides an excellent customer experience.

6. It could be used for authentication to all self-service channels.

Although it is a good solution, VB has also some drawbacks like false accept and false reject rates. As the technology develops, the accuracy of VB systems are getting better and significant progress has been achieved in recent years and somewhere around 96% + accuracy has been achieved. If you compare this figure with other biometric tools applicability to your client base (for example, only iPhone 6 users with the knowledge & experience of using Touch ID), you may conclude that VB is in the second rank just after SMS in terms of adaptability to a large sample of clients. Accuracy of Voice Biometric

Authentication heavily depends on reducing background noise - vendors know this and are working on it, significant progress has been achieved so far.

There are some other factors that should be considered when selecting a VB tool. For example, Local language support is required and very critical, together with how you enrol your clients – these make a huge difference. Also, something called "aliveness detection" is important, a pre-recorded voice or a robotic one should not be authenticated by VB controls. Of course, regulations and privacy concerns should also be taken into consideration too.

IN A NUTSHELL

Among all the other biometric solutions, Voice Biometrics (VB) has a special advantage: Convenience! It works with every mobile device (smart. dumb, expensive and cheap) plus even with landlines. Plus minimum user participation is required.

## CHAPTER 18

## TIP EIGHTEEN: LOCATION BASED SERVICES

"My grandmother started walking five miles a day when she was sixty. She's ninety-seven now, and we don't know where the hell she is." *Ellen DeGeneres*

When "Location Based Services (LBS)" and "Banking" terms meet, usually the very first thing that comes to mind is Branch / ATM finders on the websites. Actually LBS have much more potential than this for digital banking, especially when the mobile devices are added to the party.

"Knowing where the customer is" is a very powerful information tool when used well. Some of the potential benefits LBS might bring to the banking are context based marketing, capturing client's behavioral data, increasing security and providing a base for Value Added Service for SME (small & medium Enterprise) companies - who are bank's business customers too.

Let's start with how LBS data is collected, broadly speaking there are five ways:

1. **On Device GPS tools:** accessed by the bank's native app, so GPS based location is acquired via internet by your bank (HTML 5 also provides location info too.)

2. **GSM Networks:** used data captured by GSM Operators and shared with your bank.

3. Connected Wi-Fi locations: sometimes tell the story.

4. Not very commonly used, but **Self-Reporting positioning** can be done by clients manually.

5. **Proximity Based communications:** like Bluetooth, Infrared and Near Field technologies share locations of the clients too.

It is possible to categorize LBS into two forms: **INDOOR** and **OUTDOOR**. If the LBS info tells you the location of a Shopping Mall - this is outdoor. If the LBS info tells you Starbucks is on the second floor, north east of the mall - this is indoor. Proximity marketing, ibeacons and in store marketing, all rely on indoor marketing. That's why both Apple and Google invest so much (especially in the form of purchasing new companies – another quick tip, if you're wondering where technological trends are headed, check out what companies Apple

& Google are acquiring!) in this area.

As you might guess, the most essential part and first step of LBS is to position your bank's assets into the map in the most accurate way. There are some tools available, to position even free format addressed in to the map in a very short time (how about calibrating and locating one million free format addresses in one day, I saw it – then bought the tool!) This process is called calibration.

Most banks use their own maps in the local servers, but it is advisable to use some well-known map applications like Google, Yandex or Bing also. If you want to use these type of maps you either need to work with the map provider directly, or their local official partners in your area (yes, you need to pay too!) It is important to note that a majority of map searches are done in these maps, so it is more likely that your clients will use Google and Yandex to find you rather than your own map (unless your mobile app is sexy enough to be used for map searches too.) Also, GPS navigations and other parties would rely on this data - so you better position yourself in one of those map providers. I already observed very accurate positioning (max 3 meter inaccuracy) is possible. Also please note that regular updates of your bank's positions is a legal and business requirement too.

After the basic introduction to LBS, you might like to know that your bank can use it.

I assume you have heard about the Gold Rush in Alaska from late 1800's to early 1900's. There were thousands of gold diggers who went there to find their fortune. Most of these people were disappointed, but a merchant named Levi Strauss used the Gold Rush as an opportunity to introduce and sell a new form of clothing called jeans - that were durable (do you know that the oldest known pair of Levi's jeans were found in 1997 and were 100 years old. So the guy did the job well!) And were resistant to water – they were sold to gold diggers and Strauss made a fortune. In other words, he became a facilitator and created his own goldmine.

Banks can become LBS facilitators for their SME (I love SME's, they are the main growth engine of the economy and main job providers: from China to US) clients, give a hand to them and place their locations (you have their addresses right?) into calibrated maps on behalf of them. Then via bank apps - direct customers to these places, for shopping – via campaigns and special discounts depending on the agreement between the bank and merchant. When users request a restaurant or a service, your POS merchants might get a priority listing, or when someone is looking for a special service, like a health service or car rental - you might advise your card/loyalty program benefits to go to preferred locations.

It is also possible to provide an online campaign management dashboard for each merchant; so that they can enter their own campaigns. (Imagine the merchant has low sales on one day or would like to get rid of the excess inventory stock. (So he has a motivation to use the app!) For your banks credit cards. They sell; you get the commission and clients are satisfied. So it is a three wins result: win (bank) – win (merchant) and win (client.))

Facebook, Foursquare, Google places and Yelp are the most common applications - in which you should have ownership of your domains. When your customers check in (means when they say that they are there) - you can inform them that there are some special discounts to your bank's credit card, or an immediate personal loan for the TV set sold in store X, or maybe at the airport, tell them how to find your bank's lounge. Let's go for more fantastic offers, how about offering travel insurance if they login to digital banking with their white listed (as usual) device?

Using LBS for competitor's analysis is another cool thing we have done. I have been talking about something like checking out where the competitor branches / ATMs (and recent openings) then use this information for new branch/ATM openings. If you ever played "Sim City" and "Capitalism" PC games, more or less the idea is the same – just as if you played both games together, at the same time!

Location Based Services can be used for security too. Recently, card providers started to compare client's location (via GSM signals) and where the card was used for shopping. If there is a difference, then they block the transaction for fraud suspicion. (However, this does not solve the BUYER and PAYER dilemma - the ones who have kids know what mean, right?!) In the same way, many bank's Fraud Detection Systems compares the current login attempt with previous ones. If there is an impossible travel distance between two places with a first login from Istanbul, and the next one from Toronto in two hours - on the assumption that legitimate clients do not play with VPNs while banking, or share their credentials with others (or the client is not the **Raymond Reddington** from Blacklist who regularly changes his private jet direction in the air and rarely goes where planned to!) blocks the login too.

Another area is using augmented reality to impress your clients. If you wonder what it is, it basically means that your client looks to the world from the window of his phone's camera then sees that elephants dancing, rabbits singing and your Branches/ATMs shining with how to get there instructions!

Some typical questions that might come to mind,

## Tolga Tavlas

regarding personal use of LBS:

> **1st** question: "is it possible to fool location based systems about your location?" the answer is YES - but don't trust this, as it depends on who wants to find you!

> **2nd** question: "is it possible to track your location when your phone is switched off?" the answer is YES - the capabilities of our mobile devices on or off - are pretty amazing!

So LBS are the basis for proximity marketing and mobile payments, which would be the future of marketing in my opinion.

IN A NUTSHELL

As you might guess, the most essential part and first step of LBS is to position your bank's assets into the map in the most accurate way.

## CHAPTER 19

## TIP NINETEEN: SOCIAL MEDIA

**"It may be a coincidence that the decline of newspapers has corresponded with the rise of social media. Or maybe not."**
**Ryan Holmes**

Digital transformation created two segments of people in society: **Digital Natives** (technologists) and **Digital Immigrants** (adapters). From the banking perspective, the change in customer behavior, together with technological transformation (mobile, social media, wearables etc.) - necessitates adaptation to this new environment. As the majority of top banking managers are Digital Immigrants, they ask for help from Digital Natives (mostly either young talents of the bank or external companies/agents) how to manage this change. Of course there is a strategic gap between the two minds. Even so, resources were allocated, money spent, resulting in a million-plus followers on Social Media, but ... no idea what to do with them!

A majority of banks are managed by using traditional KPIs (Key Performance Indicators) and ROIs (Return of Investment) - from the management perspective, it is always good to know "how can we measure the success and how much you put in / how much you get out?" On the other side, if KPI or ROI of Social Media activities are considered, things get a little bit complicated. You can find a couple of KPI/ROI definitions for SM and depending on the channel, it varies (if it is YouTube, how many times it was watched and liked, Twitter Followers, Facebook likes etc.) but the principle is the same. Unfortunately, none of the Social Media KPIs are anything close to what "digital immigrant" bankers look for. They need something like "you managed to sell X number of items thanks to Social Media, or this SM activity contribution to revenue is Y%. Unless you provide transactional banking services on social media, like some banks do, you can not get these KPIs. I think providing banking services in social media is a little bit of a tricky issue, it certainly has a strong marketing gimmick (which is where the customer is) but its effectiveness, security and compliance is controversial.

In my opinion, Banks cannot compete with disruptors by providing banking services at social media levels. What is needed is to capture the data from media about the client, process it to transform it into knowledge and then use this knowledge to produce more to the point, or relevant offers to the client. People do not mind sharing on social media, but do mind sharing with the bank (we have got some reputation issues here!) As a result, while social media companies have a 360 degree view of the client (Jack as a doctor, as a friend, as a father, as a son, as an alumni, as a husband, etc.) - we have only a tunnel vision of Jack - as he is affluent, rich or poor. So except for some valuable insight providing data, whatever Jack does in social media is none of our interest - except for magazine reasons! (as a good friend, Ted Coine said in his excellent book, "**A World Gone Social: How Companies Must Adapt to Survive**" - what happens in Vegas, stays in Vegas unless you put it on Facebook!) There are some companies who specialize in semantic analytics that are used in order to see if it is possible to understand if someone's need for extra cash, is because they are planning to buy or rent a house etc., by analyzing the social media conversations of the person. I am sure working with such companies would be much more profitable than working with Social Media brand/communication management companies.

In addition to client data gathering, there are some other areas banks might benefit from social media:

1. **CLIENT SUPPORT AND COMPLAINT MANAGEMENT** - needs a dedicated call center team and should have Service

Level Agreement with a maximum of one hour for the initial contact.

2. **CO-PRODUCT DEVELOPMENT** - organize online workshops, game like competition with clients to take their opinion about your product offerings. They are excellent mentors!

3. **MARKET BENCHMARK** - people are pretty honest (even sometimes brutal) in saying what they are thinking.

4. **BRAND MANAGEMENT (!)** - there is no such thing, you manage your brand with your business practices and social media is the mirror (actually many mirrors!) in which you can see yourself.

5. **CAMPAIGN COMMUNICATION**

communicating with the clients, preferably in a business causal - less formal way. Good sense of humor helps! (Saw some practices like client says, "I love you," bank replies, "we have feelings for you too!")

Also, it is critical to note that the Bank needs a "**How to use social media policy**" for its employees, ideally a one page maximum - written in a very plain language that tells what to do and what not to do. At the end of the day, any of you bank employees comments on a conversation can be seen as connected with your company.

As a final word, the challenge is, "how to convince

the client to give you access to his/her social ID credentials," it is not that hard - but also it is not as easy like "follow me, I will follow you." The relationship should not be one time. Instead regular communication based on transparency is required. Social Media is not a good place for any bank performing some bad business practices (like hidden fees or extra charges), as past experience showed that the punishment is very swift and strong - plus everyone watches it!

## IN A NUTSHELL

You manage your brand with your business practices and social media is the mirror (actually many mirrors!) in which you can see yourself.

## CHAPTER 20

## TIP TWENTY: BRANCHES

**"Retail banking in Africa is very weak. You can't go to a village and get money from an ATM or visit a branch of the bank. So people have to use the Internet."**
**Mo Ibrahim**

Digital Banking channels used to be called "Alternative Banking Channels" (some banks may still do that!) As the name implies, they were considered an alternative to the branches. As of today, as most transactions are handled by Digital Channels - they are not alternative anymore but the main interaction points with bank clients. In spite of big migration to Digital Channels – The branch is still where banking starts and ends for many banks. That is why the branch is still part of the Digital Banking Picture and can contribute the growth of Digital Banking.

At the time of the first introduction of online banking seventeen years ago, while we were visiting branches to explain this new channel - the very first common response we met was - "is it going to take our place?" I never believed that this would be the case, but always knew that it was the beginning of an era and nothing would be the same again. Since then, the size of branches have become smaller and branches are more sales/advisory oriented rather than operational. Also as the P/L (profit loss) metrics are very advanced now – measuring/comparing both channel and branch performance is quite easy. Depending on the bank's strategy this may result in expanding or closing the branch network, but Digital Banking is not the reason for closure, changing of the economic climate is.

Depending on the bank's dynamics, Digital channels can handle from 50% to 90% of all transactions done in the bank. This is a very huge figure. Even if online KYC is on the way and qualified digital signatures are used for account opening (using another bank for KYC by asking money transfer from another bank to your bank is another method used in some European countries) - branch is still the most dominant player for new customer on boarding for many banks. So digital channels need branches as much as branches need them in our current condition. (We may not like this but it does not change the fact that branches are still there!) Then we might wonder how can branches support the growth of Digital Channels?

Broadly speaking there are three things they can do for this purpose:

1. **AUTO ON-BOARDING:** Automatically giving Digital Banking Access to the new clients at the time of the account opening and showing them how to use it.

2. **CUSTOMER DATA QUALITY:** As they are the ones to have the first contact point with the client, who captures and enters (unless back office used) the client data into the system and data is the blood of Digital Channels, doing this task is critical.

3. **RESPONDING LEADS:** There are some initial sales activities online (if we can, we should do it fully online of course!) and the transaction is completed in the branch - which are called Leads. Finalizing these leads on time and well, should be the primary responsibility of the branches.

Bank Management is usually cautious not to create a direct competition between digital channels and branches. That is why it is very common that despite the client performing transactions online - it is recorded in the book of the branch, where the customer account is located. It is believed that by this way, branches do not mind diverting branch clients to digital channels.

At the same time, we all know that there is high sales/revenue pressure on the branches - then the question becomes, to whom are they going to sell? In the ideal world, digital channels have strong selling capabilities and as clients "go digital," they get custom & real time offers and finish the sale online via end to end procedures. However this might be the case in your bank.  So the branch's first target is to sell to the existing clients, as it is much easier than getting new ones. Then where are the existing clients? They are using Digital Channels and not visiting branches anymore - so do we really think that the branch wants this? By default NO, so we need to do something about it. How can branches be motivated to support digital?

Let's answer this question via another question: "What's in it for them?" - You need to find or create some motivations right here. First the mindset of both sides' managers should be the same (you know the story of the Mars orbiter for which NASA used the metric system, while Lockheed Martin used the English system when building it – the result was Lost in Space!)  Then you can try a couple of methods:

1. Digital Banking On-boarding could be part of their performance bonus.

2. Branch based clients penetrations are regularly measured and reported to top management.

3. You can organize campaigns for branch staff and reward the top performers.

4. You can select Digital Ambassadors for each branch and these employees will become digital representatives of the branch.

5. Regular communication (emails, road shows, meetings, etc.) with branches to increase awareness regarding the benefits of digital can be organized.

6. And the silver bullet is… whoever the most senior representative of branches in your bank (head of retail or corporate, network manager or CEO) - if you can, put the digital banking penetration ratio into his/her performance card! Actually, just do this and forget the rest! (Fire and Forget!)

Branch Call Diversions (to Contact Centers), Queue Management Systems, Alarm and Reminder Services, Online KYC (know your client) systems are all involved in the Branch - Digital Banking relationships. Sure the relationship is not an easy one, but it is something that needs to be managed.

Everyone accepts and knows that there has been a tremendous change in customer behavior in recent years, together with new business and economical conjecture. Despite branch closures in some parts of the world, I believe the digital revolution has been forcing the branches to change and transform, not become extinct.

IN A NUTSHELL

How can branches support the growth of Digital Channels?

Broadly speaking there are three things they can do for this purpose:

> ➤ Auto on-boarding
> ➤ Customer data quality
> ➤ Responding leads

## CHAPTER 21

## TIP TWENTY-ONE: CONTACT CENTER

**If it's the Psychic Network why do they need a phone number?** *Robin Williams*

One of the easiest channels to use is the Contact Center, for sure. What is required is simply dialing a few numbers – surfing through the IVR (this could be challenging though?) – finalizing your task via IVR or Agent. Contact centers are as old as Cards, so both could be considered grandparents of Digital Banking, so they deserve respect and understanding. CC business seems quite operational the task at first sight, but if used well, from improving customer satisfaction to selling products – there is a wide spectrum of benefits available. In my opinion, Contact Centers are the 911 of banking and they have a huge potential to create little miracles for the business. Also it should be noted that most of the funny and nice customer stories we hear are coming from CC too, together with painful and hard to accept ones!

First some basic introduction to Contact Center Business: CC's have both inbound and outbound capacities. Outbound is usually known as telemarketing too. In other words, sometimes Clients call CC (inbound) – sometimes CC calls clients (outbound) – for mostly support (inbound) and sales (outbound) purposes. But also please note that CC can sell via inbound calls too, after finishing the task that the client asked for – "Oh Mr/Ms X, we have a superb offer for you!" – This is what successful CC's do.

Communication with banking CC's can be done via Call, email, Social Media, online forms, fax – even on rare occasions, via printed forms. Also CC's use IVR (Interactive Voice Response) systems in order to take some work load from the agents and also directs the clients to the right way. In banking, as a rule of thumb, the functions that do not want to be found are usually hidden in the dark corners of the IVR. (Come on, don't look at me like that – you know what I mean!) The clients who want to find them either spend hours looking, or do not find them at all. So we get very angry clients (sounds like angry birds – you know the games and what angry birds do right? Now for a moment, let's imagine that the clients are angry birds and the blocks they address to be whom? Yeah true, the poor agents!) – This is no good, so better stay away from this practice.

After      the      basic      introduction let's go a

little bit deeper in the area. Contact Center businesses have many critical metrics – but seven of them are very important from a Digital Banking Perspective:

1. **Active and Waiting Calls:** (how many calls are in progress and are waiting?)

2. **Average Handling Time:** (how long does it take to solve a typical problem?)

3. **First Call Resolution / Total Problem Solutions:** (how many problems are solved on the first call and the total number of solved problems in a day?)

4. **Call Abandonment:** (how many clients called, waited – waited and waited then were disappointed and hung up?)

5. **Up Sell – Cross Sell Rate:** (Digital Channels provided the leads, but how many of those leads were turned into sales?)

6. **Cost per call:** (yeah, serving for Digital Channels has cost – usually ignored by some in the calculations of online banking cost per transaction)

7. **Revenue per call:** (the name says the story right?)

Let's look at what the Contact Centers do for Digital Banking now. Broadly speaking, CC's contribution to Digital Channels can be categorized in two headings: SUPPORT and SALES.

SUPPORT coverage can be quite large, it includes but is not limited to the items below:

> ➢ Helping Customers to explain "How to Use" or solve their problems

> ➢ Providing Customer Insight (make a guess: who knows first if there is a problem in your system? IT guys? Come on – sure first it is the customer, then? Yeah CC!)

> ➢ Complaint Management, handling and resolving the problems.

> ➢ Operational Tasks like client data update, delivering bank's key messages.

> ➢ Calling inactive (we miss you thing!) or fresh clients (welcome aboard!)

> ➢ Responding to fraud alerts, Social Media mentions, etc.

SALES is mostly related to finalizing the leads coming from Digital Channels. This can be:

> ➢ Finishing the online sales as a part of the designed processes.

> ➢ Calling back the customers who abandoned online sales forms. (That's why the very first thing you should ask in your online product application forms should be the contact details of the clients! The longer the form, the less in the sales funnel.)

> ➢ Advising clients according to rules such

as: if the client wait time is more than a predefined limit on the web page.

> ➢ Promoting online products via inbound and outbound calls.

If you want to get the benefits above, you need to motivate Call Center staff – who are usually young, energetic and hardworking people. If your digital banking channels are backed by a motivated dynamic Call Center teams – customer satisfaction levels are usually quite good. Close performance monitoring and rewarding good performance are required to set up the right balance.

As Digital Banking Channels and Call Centers are integrated so much, security of Digital Channels are also closely related with security of CC too. The last thing we want is to create a Digital Banking security perimeter where the CC is the weakest link in the chain. Some common CC authentication practices are:

> ➢ **Knowledge Based Authentication:** Usually in the form of static and dynamic questions, like client's birthday, maiden name, last spending on credit card or last account movement etc.

> ➢ **Unique Identifier and CC PIN:** Unique Identifier could be something numeric & exclusive to the client like Client Number, Citizenship/Social Security Number, Bank Account or Card Number

etc. PIN should be numeric for sure, in the form of static or dynamic (one time password.)

> **Voice Biometrics:** It could be active (that means client is asked to talk or say a specific script) or passive (at the time of the first set up the client's voice is recorded then compared with the new call.)

> **Caller ID Recognition:** Recognizing the calling number, but you cannot trust this so much especially for critical transaction requests, as the system can be fooled by the tricks of the fraudsters!

If you are interested in banking fraud business, you may know that fraudsters attack Contact Centers too – in order to modify client's information, then they use this to steal Digital Banking credentials. Therefore authenticating the client is a very important part of the Contact Center Business.

**IN A NUTSHELL**

If your digital banking channels are backed by a motivated dynamic Call Center teams – customer satisfaction levels are usually quite good. Close performance monitoring and rewarding good performance are required to set up the right balance.

## CHAPTER 22

## TIP TWENTY-TWO: ATMs

"When ATMs machines came out and people were prosecuted for robbing ATM machines, I don't think anybody thought the banks were against technology because they didn't want their ATM machines lifted." *Hilary Rosen*

ATM (automatic teller machines) is one of the most amazing banking innovations, created with the idea of providing 24 hour banking service – account checking and mostly money withdrawals. Since the first introductions of ATMs in 1960s – changing customer behaviour and expectations triggered a huge transformation for ATMs. As of today, there are more than three million ATMs used throughout the world, and Brazil is the leader with more than 160,000 machines according to the Bank Report! (seems like not only soccer but also money withdrawal from ATMs are the national sport there!) The significance for Digital Banking is obvious – as it is the only Self-Service banking channel where physical cash transactions are possible. Can ATMs do more than that for Digital Banking? The answer is YES.

ATMs are placed in the bank branches (called ON SITE) or other popular locations (called OFF Site) like airports, shopping malls or other popular sites. Advanced (multi-function) and Simple (money withdrawal only) versions of ATMs are available – usually functionality comes with a cost (you get what you paid for thing!) but technology and competition between vendors has made it possible to get a good machine at a reasonable price in recent years.

Traditionally ATMs have been used by clients with a physical card and a PIN and this is still the most common way of using ATMs but not the only one. Cardless ATM use is an option provided by some banks now. Facilitating Cardless ATM transactions could be possible first by typing a unique identifier that the client knows (Customer ID, Phone Number, Social Security No, etc.) followed by the second factor (a specific code sent to the client via SMS, One Time Password code produced by client's OTP device has or a biometric feature of the client – if the ATM has a biometric reader.)   Some banks exploit the advantage of the Cardless ATM use very well in their digital banking service benefit and provide money transfer to GSM number service.  Sure some security checks are done like first asking to type the GSM number, then the    amount and finally the security code sent to the GSM Number.

We said that some ATMs are more expensive than others because they are more advanced and powerful machines. In addition to availability of more banking services, what makes them more high end products are some extra functionalities including:

1. **Full Keyboard** – so that clients can type not only numeric but also alphabetical characters, by this way they can use some other functions like money transfers available on the ATM.

2. **Deposit / Recycled ATMs** – in the past ATMs have been used for just money withdrawal – it was a one way traffic from machine to customer. However this has changed with deposit ATMs, which allows customers to make deposits as well as withdrawals. That is important for paying bills, card payments etc. The difference between Deposit ATMs and Recycled ATMs is – from Recycled ATMs clients withdraw money, which was deposited by another client (cool isn't it?) By this way, unlike other ATMs – they do not need to be frequently visited by bank staff to replace the money cartridges.

3. **Barcode Scanning** – if your bank prints barcodes on the card statements, or the utility payment providers do that on printed or electronic bills – rather than

manually typing and following all navigation flows - your clients can show the code to the reader and immediately finalize the transaction.

4. **Biometric Readers** – if the ATM has a biometric reader (iris scanner, fingerprint or palm reader) – rather than using a physical card, your customers, without needing anything else can use the ATM only with who they are (sounds romantic! It's like "I love you for the person you are!")

5. **Dispensing out media** – this is not a very commonly used feature in banking ATMs but even so it is worth the mention due to its potential. If you want to deliver something to your clients, this could be an excellent medium. Please watch the "Automatic Thanking Machine" video on YouTube!

6. **On demand printing** – that means ATMs can print bank or card statements, contracts, transaction receipts in A4 format, etc. This may help to reduce the workload at the cashier desk too.

7. **Video Conferencing** – this feature facilitates virtual but face to face communication between the client and the dedicated agent. It could be positioned as a virtual branch, but as you may guess it would come with a significant cost!

## Tolga Tavlas

ATMs are the heavy lifters of transaction migration programs almost done by every bank in order to lower the cost to serve. The most common benefits Digital Banking channels get from ATMs are Customer GSM number updates and Using ATMs as second factors for critical transaction approvals – if the client does not have a second factor device. Digital Channels can also be promoted on ATM screens and applying for Digital Banking channel credentials via ATMs is possible too.

Furthermore, full multichannel experiences can only be achieved if customer and product journeys starts and finishes seamlessly regardless of the channel. The brain of the campaigns and customized customer offers is the CRM system. If ATMs are integrated to the CRM then client's product or service applications can start from ATMs and finish on Mobile or vice versa. For this reason, the consistency in terms of both User Experience (UX) and Design is required to provide familiarity in the eyes of the client. So we should make sure that ATMs are integrated in the right way to the Digital Banking experience – from Location Based Services to Branch/ATM locators on our website.

It should also be noted that ATMs are subject to many security threats including Physical Attacks, Card Cloning/Skimming and Customer Security (in some counties ATMs are only located inside branches to assure the security of the clients!) Also Fake ATMs were seen as result of creative criminal mind-sets too.   In some cases I observed a strong connection between ATM fraud and Digital Banking fraud – it is strongly recommended to have a Fraud System that monitors them both or separate FDS's but sharing information in real time.

## IN A NUTSHELL

ATMs are placed in the bank branches (called ON SITE) or other popular locations (called OFF Site) like airports, shopping malls or other popular sites. Advanced (multi-function) and Simple (money withdrawal only) versions of ATMs are  available – usually functionality comes with a cost.

## CHAPTER 23

## TIP TWENTY-THREE: DUMMY PHONES

**"Smartphones. Who cares? Smartphones. I only have dummy phones."** *Don Rickles*

It is very impressive to see the capabilities and possibilities that smartphones have already delivered to our lives and the potential they have. From the digital banking perspective, having a client base that use smartphones with biometric readers and know how to use every single function of the device would be very nice. However, this is rarely the case (unless your bank is located somewhere like Singapore, where the Prime Minister Posts His Own Puzzle-Solving computer code!) Actually, we have everything to be optimistic about the potential contribution of Mobile to Digital Banking; even the simplest version of mobile devices can be part of the Innovation if the business model is good.

As of today, we have various customer segments in your bank database with different understandings of "How to use Mobile." Some are power users with high end devices and can create miracles on mobile, some own smartphones but do not know how to use most of the features. Some others using phones at the basic level (SMS and Call) level etc. For this reason, we need to consider the mobile literacy variety of our client base while providing Digital Banking services to them. Most likely in a few years, there will only be smartphone owners as clients in our database and we will provide fantastic services to them by using their smartphones as tools. Until we can get there, there are some silent innovations we can do with what we have. If the alternative is to wait till the future will come and provide our services to mobile power users – then we may prefer to look for something today on mobile that could be useful for most of our clients.

Voice and SMS, also a basic camera are the most essential features every mobile phone has; either it is a smart or dumb phone (actually we should call them featured phones!)

Let's first have a closer look to SMS and how banks use it.

Very basic use of mobile phones for digital banking is digital SMS as we all know. The best thing about SMS is it works with every phone; smart or dumb phone difference makes no sense for SMS. What kinds of roles are given to SMS by Digital Banking?

> **Critical information delivery:** (Like One Time Password or Activation Code.)

> **Client information confirmation:** (Client applies for a product and you send SMS to check validity of the contact information.)

> **Security Alerts:** (Money Comes / goes alerts, credit card spending.)

> **Value Added Services:** (Stock prices that you watch Increased / dropped a predefined limit)

> **Campaign Management:** (calls or location based supported.) Not bad for a 160 character dummy message, is it?

For These Reasons, banks love SMS - so it is guaranteed to work with every device and goes to the right person via closed network (GSM). On the downside, it is not free. (Do not be mean to GSM operators, the money lost due to WhatsApp & similar message services already hurts them emotionally!) And it is not very secure (SMS forwarders are a common threat, but for Smartphones, no threat for dumb ones). When the banks compared advantages with disadvantages, the conclusion seems like going with it...

The other basic use of mobile phone is Voice transfer – that is the basis of verbal communication (some says that 90% of the communication is non-verbal but this is another story!) If we ask ourselves how we can use this function - the answer is utilizing it for Voice Biometrics!

Voice biometrics is one of the most interesting security topics on the rise. It usually works in real time and provides quite a low number of false positives (false accept or false reject) thanks to recent developments in voice recognition technology. If you get your client's voiceprint at the time of the enrollment, that would be enough to use it for actively (you can ask) or passively (listen in the background) for client authentication. All that is needed is a phone with a microphone – that means almost all of your clients can use Voice biometric services.

I think the camera function might be considered as a basic mobile functionality too. There are many Digital On boarding services using mobile for Online KYC (know your client) via mobile device cameras – you can position mobile phones for picture based authentication tools too. Of course you cannot rely on this only but this would be a security check if you need to verify the client ID.

In sum, the smarter the phone, the more functionality available, but still even the most basic phone functions could be useful for Digital Banking. SMS, Voice and Camera functionalities of the devices are something you rely on and can be used by most of your clients. Think about the mobile banking revolution in Africa – did it start with cutting edge smartphones or power mobile users?

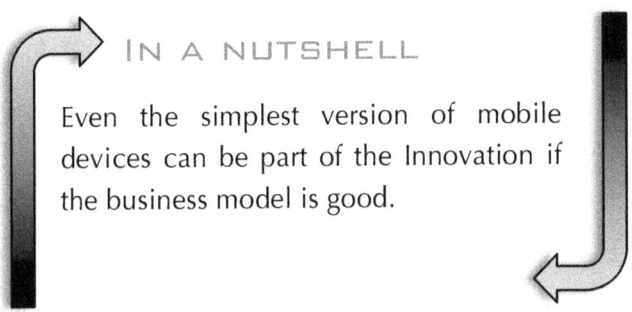

IN A NUTSHELL

Even the simplest version of mobile devices can be part of the Innovation if the business model is good.

## CHAPTER 24

## TIP TWENTY-FOUR: ALARM AND REMINDER SERVICES

**"If you do build a great experience, customers tell each other about that. Word of mouth is very powerful."** *Jeff Bezos*

Alarm and Reminder (or notification) services may be seen or positioned as a separate financial product, but in fact they are quite important for digital banking. The prerequisite of providing this service is to have the client's valid contact information (email or GSM number, ideally both) or your bank's mobile application should be installed in the client's mobile device. The information may be sent to the client (push) or client may ask for it (pull) by sending a message and asking for the information (like account inquiry).

Broadly speaking, Alarm and Reminder service means that sending an alert - mostly in the form of SMS, email, Wireless Application Protocol, Push - to the customer based on a trigger. So what could be the trigger? There are two main categories of trigger as Rule Based and Time Based. If a certain action or condition is required for sending Alerts - this is **Rule Based**. For example, money comes to or leaves from an account, unusual spending on a credit card, end of time deposit, price increase of a selected stock, etc., could be the reasons for sending alerts. The other type is, celebrating the client's birthday, reminding a payment or taxes due date (oh clients love this!) – This is **Time Based**.

Alarm and Reminder services can be provided as free of charge or on a fixed fee - depending on the bank's preference. (Together with what local banking authorities think about the fee thing). The biggest advantage of this service is REDUCING the branch and call center calls. As it does not require technical knowledge (whether we like it or not - there are still some groups of customer segments that consider using online or mobile banking as rocket science!) and works with almost every device. It also gives a sense of control to the clients so that increases customer satisfaction.

Then the question is how to engage the customer in this service? If it is a fee based service, you can create some bundles or sell with another product. Something like an Investment Package, Accounts Package etc.

If it is a free service, it makes your job much easier - typically free services use email and wireless application protocol push due to cost reasons - automatically opt in everyone and tell them if they want, they can opt out! As this is not a marketing thing, you would be surprised to learn that more than 90% of clients will keep on using it. Also, engagement to Alarm and Reminder services should be as auto-on boarding when the client opens an account in your bank. So starting from day one, your clients would subscribe to such a nice service.

Here's a checklist for Alarm Reminder Services, please ask these questions to yourself – I believe your answers will help you to position these services in the most appropriate way at your bank:

1. Which Alarm / Reminder Services does your bank provide? (credit cards, accounts, investments, etc.) And which ones are most frequently used?

2. Why does a typical Retail Client receive SMS/ email /PUSH from your bank and how often?

3. Is the business model of A/R sustained as COST SAVING or REVENUE GENERATION item? Why?

4. How are A/R services positioned – is it supplementary to Digital Banking or an alternative?

5. What is the penetration of Alarm/Reminder services?

6. What is the (estimated) percentage of (%) clients – who gave their GSM numbers and emails to the bank? Which channel/s are used to gather this information?

7. Which services are charged (How is pricing done, who pays for the SMS?) Are any bundles or packages sold?

8. Is it a pull & push service – is the service automated and/or triggered by the client?

9. Which channels are used to initiate and manage the service settings?

10. Are there any business initiative / departments that encourages the use of this service?

11. Do you have a centralized communication tool/software that manages all communication with the customers, like an email marketing tool – SMS sender system – Social Media Manager etc.

12. What type of reporting infrastructure is used to measure the performance of the A/R Services and can you see the details of the numbers (clients using the service, penetrations, etc.)

13. Does it require signing a new contract to use this service or does the current banking contract cover the use of this service?

14. Are there any pre-defined sets (packages)

for A/R Services or do customers need to define the items individually?

15. Do your competitors provide such a service? If yes, what type of A/R services are used and which services are provided? Do they charge any fees for this service?

16. Can auto-on boarding be done or is there a limit that stops this action? For example, is it possible to on-board everyone to A/R email service – send an email to inform them and give an opt-out option?

17. Which Credit Cards and SECURITY functions/features are required to contact with the client and how often?

One quick experience to share: imagine the ATM took your card while you were trying to withdraw some cash at midnight. You are nervous as you do not know if this is a card copy trick or a technical problem - and you don't know what to do. At the moment of need, you receive a SMS from your bank that says everything is under control - they know why this happened and your card is not stolen, but kept by the bank. This is what Alarm and Reminder services can do for you – provide seamless customer experience...

## IN A NUTSHELL

Alarm and Reminder services (also known as notifications) means that sending an alert - mostly in the form of SMS, email, WAP, Push - to the customer based on a trigger.

CHAPTER 25

"Great companies that build an enduring brand have an emotional relationship with customers that has no barrier. And that emotional relationship is on the most important characteristic, which is trust."
Howard Schultz

Social CRM has been one of the hot topics for banking in recent years, especially after the strong surge of Social Media, which has taken a place in our daily lives. From the banking point of view, it represents the change from marketing to engagement, in terms of customer relationship management. While Traditional CRM is fed by the customer data inside the bank, Social CRM's fuel has been coming from Social Media, where our customers share their data publicly and generously. If you need to make a choice between two CRMs, go for Social CRM – as it is much more entertaining (don't you want to know what your clients eat, drink, wear and the places they visit?) and informative.

As we all know in times past, the relationship between the bank and client was quite different than it is today. In the past, conversation was often one-sided with the bank driving the dialogue while the customers listened. (*It's a Wonderful Life! – the Holiday drama movie produced in 1946 and it was about community banking!*). After digitalization created a power shift from bank to the client, the roles have reversed and it is the bank's turn now to listen to what customers say. So Social CRM concepts have been introduced into our lives by the digital transformation.

In the simplest terms, "Social CRM is Customer Relationship Management through social media." Twitter, Facebook or any other similar social media channels could be the platform to facilitate such communication. Customer Engagement and Interaction are two of the most important components of Social CRM, which are used to gain knowledge about the client. Unlike Traditional CRM (T-CRM), Social CRM (S-CRM) is not limited to the data stored in the bank's database, and goes beyond what a bank can collect in "business as usual" methods and technologies. So the nature of the client relation is not transaction, but interaction.

Social CRM also represents a change in the business mind set.

Let me explain what I mean with this. Sales,

## Tolga Tavlas

Marketing and Support are the three components of Traditional CRM; the missing parts are Customer Experience and Customer Advocacy. Plus, T-CRM assumes that a Bank's reputation/brand is managed by PR or Communication departments – not clients. Using S-CRM means that accepting the change in the banking landscape and adapting this, as well. Currently, rather than increasing budgets for internal PR activities, investing in online communities in order to convert followers to customers and advocates, is much more reasonable option for the banks. This is much more effective and efficient than the traditional way (no insult to PR colleagues). If not convinced, try to get some business insight from your few thousand clients in just 24 hours!

Listening to what customers think about the bank's products and services is the asset S-CRM brings to the table. Then the interaction with clients would follow. Banks should talk with clients just as they do with each other. The influence of a client in the digital economy cannot be measured or understood by checking the net value s/he has in your bank. (*Have you ever thought about how a mass client in your bank might also be a private client of your competitor's, and how can you discover this information?*) Social CRM might help you find out some information that cannot be found in traditional ways.

**The fuel of Social CRM,** as you guess, is: **DATA**. Where does this data come from? Digital Analytics.

In tip 20, we have talked about Digital Analytics in detail – that requires gathering information about your client via web, mobile and social media outlets. The goal is to use such data to create a customer driven channel experience. In other words, in today's banking world, we should let the client drive the banking experience and regularly interact with the bank. Hopefully, at the end the day this will create some recommendations about your bank's products and services to others. (*I could use the cliché, "customers listen other customers more than the companies that make the product selection," come on guys you already know that don't you?!*)

I have always been surprised with how generously people share their private lives in Social Media – like a kind of dance where nobody's watching thing! Of course you do not need to listen all conversation (*if aunt Selma's coming to visit for Xmas, it's none of our business – well... maybe selling a travel insurance to Selma could be good idea, but anyway...),* you should only listen to what is relevant. This would be the base for "insight on demand," also the source of innovation.

**TEXT or SENTIMENT ANALYTICS** might give you an idea if the potential client has been looking for some money, or about to buy a car or house, loves travelling, possibly changing jobs, etc. Don't get me wrong, I don't mean you should spy on clients – this should be done with the consent or permission based information exchange (or marketing) of course. (*Except for couple of recent banking scandals, most of the banking business is still legitimate isn't it?!*). There are some tools that might help to surface the best signals for banking needs and predicting the next best action for your clients. If you want to have a real S-CRM, you better have these tools in your perimeter.

In another tip (Tip 4 – Banks and Social Media), I have mentioned what is needed is to capture the data from media about the client, process it to transform it into useable knowledge and then use this knowledge to produce the most relevant offers to the client. Also Client Support and Complaint Management, Co-Product Development and Brand Management are the other areas Social CRM can help.

I always consider CRM and Fraud Detection Tools (FDS) as two sides of the same coin. Like FDS tools, your S-CRM should learn from experience and work on based on these rules. That means the accumulated customer insight must help create more targeted engagement opportunities as time passes. Also, you need to know what the last contact with the client was and keep track of all communications you have had in the past. (If the client complains about X on twitter, you don't want to insist on doing the same thing again and again, right?)

It is also critical to note that the relationship should not be one time. Instead regular communication based on transparency is required. If you want to build trust between your bank and your clients, you need to know them. In other words, if you know what they are talking about – you have a chance to produce relevant products and services for them. This is the only way of producing a seamless omnichannel experience for your clients.

Oh, also please do not forget to reward your loyal customers!

### IN A NUTSHELL

It is a surprising fact that people generously share their private lives on Social Media, a kind of dance like nobody's watching thing! Social CRM can help you gather this data, of course, always with client consent.

## CHAPTER 26

## TIP TWENTY-SIX: BIG DATA

"We Facebook users have been building a treasure lode of Big Data that government and corporate researchers have been mining to predict and influence what we buy and for whom we vote. We have been handing over to them vast quantities of information about ourselves and our friends, loved ones and acquaintances."
**Douglas Rushkoff**

"BIG DATA" is one of the most famous Digitalization concepts in recent years. Not only in the financial landscape, but also in most other industries too. Everyone talks about it and mentions how important it is, but except for a few, many do not know what to do with it. As the 90% of the world's data generated over the last two years and has been getting bigger each and every second, using the Big Data in an efficient way is a critical success factor for banking business. Considering that banks have been sitting on a data gold mine, we have substantial capacity to turn Big Data into knowledge that can be used to unlock new revenue opportunities.

Digitalization brought so many things into our lives, numbers have been flying around – we've almost lost our sense of reality due to the tremendous changes we've experienced. Let me explain in this way: one of the greatest writers in history was William Shakespeare (*it was rumoured that the guy had 15,000 words capacity when a typical Englishman spoke up to 1,000 words, while the elite used 3,000 in the 1600s*). Every sonnet, poem and play written by Shakespeare – when scanned, is around 5MB. This is quite less than a digital native youngster can produce in just a few minutes, isn't it? Please do not get me wrong, we only compare in terms of data size, not content!

After digitalization, there have been some major changes in the banking space:

> It has never been more competitive than it is today.

> We have been competing not only with banks but also non-financial new players as well.

> Customer behaviours and expectations have changed.

> Mobile is quickly becoming the primary channel of banking - that helps both information gathering and pushing offers.

There has also been a clear shift from transactional banking to relationship driven banking. Therefore; changing the nature of the banking landscape pushes banks to create more operationally efficient business models and create new customer segments or markets.

Almost everyone believes that Big Data analytics offer a significant competitive advantage and this would be the critical success factor in the future. So, it seems that what needs to be done is obvious, following the question how this would be done. From the banking perspective, BIG DATA may help us in three main categories:

1. Obtaining new clients,

2. Increasing our share of the wallet,

3. Keeping our existing customers.

One way or another, banks should learn how to profit from big (and getting bigger) volumes of customer data. If we know more about our clients, it would be easier to find out "the RIGHT PRODUCT for the RIGHT CLIENT at the RIGHT TIME." This will also facilitate a seamless banking experience and a strong relationship with our customers – the result is: trust & confidence.

There are a few banks which have done an excellent job in putting Big Data into practice, while the majority is still thinking about it or working on small pilot projects. Single customer view or Data Silos in the bank databases do not make things easier, obviously, but this cannot be a valid excuse not to use such a valuable tool like Big Data. If we have been looking for a risk, losing market share and being unprofitable are much bigger ones than not knowing what to do with Big Data. We should see it as an opportunity, which might be useful for:

1. Acquiring new clients.

2. Risk Management and Reducing payment and digital banking frauds.

3. Increasing revenue by offering targeted and personalized products to the clients.

4. Predicting the next best actions of our clients in order to give them what they need.

5. Reducing churn by making the right moves to stop our clients before they leave.

6. Increasing Client Satisfaction by improving our relationships with them.

7. Getting a full (360 degree) view of our clients, not a single one – removing the silos!

8. Supporting our bank staff to make the right decisions about client actions.

9. Improving Call Center efficiency.

10. Creating new Customer Segmentations to

## Tolga Tavlas

better serve the changing expectations,

11. Higher customer loyalty based on trust and confidence – that means a bigger share of the wallet and greater customer lifetime value.

We cannot deny the fact that Big Data sets are pretty complex, expensive to store and analyze, it also requires some new skills in the bank and client privacy should be taken into consideration. At the same time, we can manage this. If Big Data is positioned as a strategic priority (*please do not call it a project, as it is NOT a project – it has no start and no finish, it is an ongoing thing!*) – Then none of these challenges can be a problem.

It is pretty obvious that unless we find or create new services and revenue streams (that means adaptation to the new economy), banks run the risk of losing up to 50 % market share to the new digital competitors - in five years! BIG DATA could be one of the most important assets banks have to regain the lost territory, if used well.

## IN A NUTSHELL

BIG DATA may help us in three main categories:

1. Obtaining new clients,

2. Increasing our share of the wallet,

3. Keeping our existing customers.

## CHAPTER 27

**"You have to learn the rules of the game. And then you have to play better than anyone else."**
**Albert Einstein**

"GAMIFICATION" means making the services or products more enjoyable and motivating for the users. Considering that BANKING is not the most entertaining industry in the eyes of the majority, bankers should work harder to deploy principles of Gamification in Banking. However, this could be done there are both success stories and failures. The goal is to increase customer engagement, then raise the loyalty among clients and increase the customer's lifetime value. If you'd like to know what differentiates losers from winners, keep on reading.

Gamification is not something unfamiliar to banking in general, but early examples were not like the ones used today and those were mostly initiated not by the banks. The very first gamification in a banking example was with Charles Floyd (also called Pretty Boy) – an American bank robber who lived during the Great Depression. He endeared himself to the public by destroying mortgage papers at the banks he robbed, freeing many from their debts. *(A quick note:* During his crime spree, bank insurance rates in Oklahoma were reported to have doubled. So no one can deny the positive effect created for insurance business. By the way, *a bank robbery is only classified as such if it takes place within office hours, when people are present. If there is no threat against a person the perpetrators are classed as burglars.*) I guess you might imagine how popular he was in the minds of many, as the "Pretty Boy" was seen as the "Robin Hood of the Cookson Hills." Of course this is a bad example and not one created by the banks.

At present, there are good examples of gamification in banking, created by banks for the purpose of:

1. Marketing and Retention

2. Customer Engagement

3. Co-product development (producing ideas)

4. Providing Education and Training (to educate your clients on a product or service or explain banking concepts to a new generation).

5. Increasing Employee Productivity

6. Creating Crowdfunding projects

7. Increasing client loyalty

8. Encouraging customers to spend more time on bank's digital perimeters

9. Reputation thanks to virality

*Interest* is one of the most commonly used terms in banking, in different places for different reasons. Gamification has been a popular topic for the last five years and the core idea behind it is gaining clients' interest. In other words, you will use gamification to influence your clients. How? Using gaming principles and techniques, which includes but is not limited to: competition, achievement, learning and more. Gamification could be an excellent tool not only for addressing clients but also employees.

If BIG DATA is involved in the game, Gamification works even better. Since you know about your audience behaviors, preferences and interests – you may produce much more relevant offerings – right? When you reach such a level, I mean using Big Data for such people, then you highly deserve to be in the "A" league of Banking. Considering that many banks cannot gain more than basic descriptive items about their clients, knowing 360 degrees of your client's life deserves praise.

As is the case for all games, there should be a GOAL sustained by a set of actions. Think about Monopoly.

*(There are many people who learned mathematics with this game at a very young age, loved this game and tried to use the same principles in life. Some made lots of money from estates until the subprime mortgage crisis!)* The idea is to become the richest player in the game and own all the property on the table. In order to do this you need to buy and rent, and stay out of jail etc. In your game, you will decide the goal and set of actions, but this is not easy. You need to create something engaging, fun and entertaining. Let's accept the fact that these are not ours (bankers) strongest assets! So most of the time, web agencies with strange senses of humour design these games and banks pay for it. Some become successful, most do not.

Success comes from analysing best practices, understanding your clients, and knowing what you want to do.

Personally, I have never seen a bank that provides horrible online user experience but excellent games. Also it is critical to note that gamification does not come as free, you need to pay to develop and maintain. Once I was involved in a gamification project several years ago for a mortgage project and developed some awards for the winners. The result was a total disappointment: Rather than the targeted segment of people – we ended up with professional game players in Social Media. You might be very surprised to see the total     number of IDLE people

# Tolga Tavlas

in the social media jungle waiting for an opportunity to win something free! So, uncle Tolga says that not every gamification project is good, unless you set your goals clearly and know what you're doing – you have a very limited chance to succeed in this task.

As of today, banks focus more on motivating clients to spend or save money through gamification. So whatever the targeted behaviour of the client is, the games can be produced to sustain this purpose. There should be some challenges on the way and the users should be rewarded with points or badges. Also, as always, we human beings have a strong tendency to compare ourselves with others – you should bet on this as well by adding some components that facilitates competition with other clients. As the idea creates a viral effect, you better install social components so your clients share their success stories or formulas on social media. Also; when designing a game, you must also think about which platform would be used to play this game. PC, Mobile/tablet or any other online or offline platforms.

According to some research (coming from a popular research group), 70% of the top 2000 companies in the world have had at least one gamification app in their perimeter in the last five years. However, (it sounds a little bit oxy-moronic) the very same research company also declared that 80 Percent of these gamified applications failed to meet business objectives primarily due to poor design. So basic statistics say that we have 1400 top companies in hand and 1,120 of them had miserable gamification experiences due to poor design. Well, frankly blaming only design for such a failure is a little bit unfair – as I am a firm believer that the ugliest designed web sites are the ones that make the most money (such as Google, Yahoo and eBay!).

Just think about it...

## IN A NUTSHELL

As of today, banks focus more on motivating clients to spend or save money through gamification. So whatever the targeted behaviour of your client is, games can be produced to sustain this purpose.

## CHAPTER 28

## TIP TWENTY-EIGHT: ARTIFICIAL INTELLIGENCE

**"There are some ideas so wrong that only a very intelligent person could believe in them."**
**George Orwell**

As of today, the banking industry has been experiencing the most challenging times in its history because of Digital Disruption. Every banker agrees that there is a great risk of losing market share against new Fintech players, which means losing customers, profit and staff soon. Artificial or not, we all need intelligence for sure – as soon as possible. As described by Stephen Hawking, "Intelligence is the ability to adapt to change" and this is what banks need desperately. Then the question is: how can Artificial Intelligence (AI) help banks to become and stay more competitive?

It might be good to start with the definition of Artificial Intelligence (AI) – in the simplest terms it means the intelligence shown by machines or software. You probably heard about more fantastic names given to AI like "machine learning," "smart machines" or "cognitive computing" – broadly speaking they all refer to the same efforts coming from the 1950s to make smarter machines in the form of smart algorithms.

If you are like me and not involved much in the scientific side of AI business, probably the very first experience you had with AI is from the TERMINATOR movies when you were young. A killing robot vs a decent robot (Arnold Schwarzenegger), called Terminator (a weird name for a decent robot). He was a human-looking indestructible cyborg is sent from 2029 to 1984 (by the way, seems like we've still got several years to go to reach 2029 and find out where Cyborg is – the name sounds like an Austrian town doesn't it?). Things have changed a lot in the Artificial Intelligence area over the last ten years especially in the movie business. If you watched the movie, "HER" that is about a romantic relationship between a man and an Operating System! (By the way it was one of the most romantic films I have ever seen, no joke!) You may fully see the picture that shows where we are going. (But nothing compares to Austin Powers' Fembots and his famous Fembot Dance!)

When you google on the net about Artificial Intelligence (AI), there are very interesting stories about Hitchhiking Robots, 3D Printer

# Tolga Tavlas

Tattoo Machines, Foodie Chef truck of IBM and many others. Artificial Intelligence is from the same family as BIG DATA and DATA ANALYTICS (if you have not read the tips about these two yet, you may like to give a try) – when you use one, you need the others.

How about us? How have banks been using Artificial Intelligence (AI) for daily business? Operational Efficiency and Cost Saving looks like the major motivations on the banking side to go for AI. At present, banks do not have Physical AI robots (except for the Bank of Tokyo, they have one cute robot called, Nao, who greets everyone in the branch. Unlike what you assumed, it was not built by a Japanese company, but a French one! By the way, there is a cutting edge tech robot in the bank, but customers still go to branches to meet him – ironic isn't it?) But there are many Software AI robots that have been used by the banks all around the globe for the purpose of:

> ➢ Personalizing Financial Services – based on data and best practices.

> ➢ Credit Card and Digital Banking Fraud Monitoring, Management and Response – the base is predicting the irregular activities.

> ➢ Providing                                  Voice Assisted Banking Services

> ➤ Supporting Decision Making Processes

> ➤ Contact Center Customer Interactions (either as chatbots or knowledge base support to the agents)

> ➤ Stock Trading Activities

> ➤ Monitoring clients' spending habits and patterns, and using this data for X and Up-Sell.

> ➤ Fund/Portfolio Management of their clients, suggesting investment strategies on changing marketing conditions.

> ➤ Advising clients for decision making, at the same time guiding bank staff how to set up the customer interaction.

> ➤ Performing repetitive tasks and improving standardization.

As banking databases are full of Descriptive Data, unless this data is replaced by Behaviour Based Data – Artificial Intelligence's contribution to banking is very much limited. (Imagine you have a Volkswagen diesel car but you put gasoline into the tank – what happens? Yes, that's right – you get much lower emission rates provided that you have a nice software installed in the car!) Fresh and Dynamic data is required for AI, then it will take care of the rest.

In the future, rather than asking human experts – questions will be asked to machines by the management of the banks for cost and effectiveness reasons. It might sound a little bit irritating, but it is obvious that there would be many banking jobs done by machines in very near future. Currently, the total size of investment portfolios managed by Robo-Advisers is around $2.3 billion in USD and there are more than 200 Robo-advice platforms in the US only. Many banks use them for their new generation of clients, unlike the old timers – millennials are much happier with them.

Even the modest estimations say that the banking industry will be using Robots widely, so from a banking employer point of view: not only Fintech companies but also AI systems could be threat to job security. Of course, there are some components of banking that cannot be replaced by algorithms – even so, the room for humans would be very limited in financial advice areas, in my opinion.

There are smart applications of AI in Insurance business as well, if your bank is interested in Insurance you may like to have a look to Insurance underwriting AI systems that automate the underwriting process and utilize more granular information to make better decisions.

The key characteristic of AI systems is their capacity to reason, gather and concentrate information, perceive examples, learn and adjust to new circumstances or environments. Mobile Banking

Apps or Mobile Wallets provided by the banks are key elements to gather the behavioural data needed by AI systems. So we should expect direct integration of banking channels with AI systems and mutually influence each other.

### IN A NUTSHELL

Unless Descriptive Data in the banking databases is replaced by Behaviour Based Data – Artificial Intelligence's contribution to banking becomes limited. It is also critical to know that Big Data and Data Analytics are the core components needed for AI.

## ABOUT THE AUTHOR

Tolga Tavlas has been acknowledged throughout his seventeen year career as a customer-centric, analytical leader and trouble-shooter. He is a world-class professional with progressive digital business experience, accumulated at consulting and financial services firms in Europe and Turkey. He is an expert at conceiving and implementing digital solutions. These cost-effective solutions have proven to elevate brand image, maximize online security, and generate revenues.

Tolga attended Middle East Technical University, graduating as an honour student with a BA in Sociology. He continued his education and graduated with distinction from the University of Leicester, with a Master's degree in Criminology and Internet Security. Later he attended the INSEAD Executive Education Program. Tolga began his career as a System Analyst at the Ottoman Bank in Istanbul, Turkey. He spent time in Ireland as a Senior Business Analyst and Consultant for Dretec Software and returned to Turkey as Project Consultant for the British Council before moving on as Project Manager for the Anadolubank.

Tolga started at Yapi Kredi as Head of the Internet Banking Department and was promoted to Digital Channels Director. Accountable for the performance of the bank's digital banking channels, at all times his goal was to improve customer service quality and build relationships.

Tolga's strength lies in his ability to translate broad strategies into clear objectives and practical action plans. During his time at Yapi Kredi, their Digital Banking Channels won many prestigious awards and was named Best Internet and Mobile Banking in Turkey and Europe many times.

Tolga has taken a turn on the speaking stage as well; lecturing on Mobile Security at Bilgi University and presenting at eCrime and Digital Banking Congresses and events in different parts of the world.

Currently Tolga is the Digital Banking and Cyber Security Expatriate for CEE RETAIL, UniCredit Bank

Austria AG. His role is to support the bank in moving clients from traditional banking channels to digital services. He is responsible for delivering digital insight among twelve Central and Eastern Europe countries and creating new interactions between internet banking and mobile channels to produce a seamless Omni-channel experience. Tolga also specializes in cyber-security, coordinating business and security units and providing concrete recommendations for mitigating threats.

When not fighting cybercrime, Tolga enjoys baroque music, photography, chess, and travel. He considers himself a lifelong learner and writes a blog at Finextra, which has captured a great deal of attention from the banking community - affording him the honor of becoming one of the top bloggers of the digital banking arena.

# THANK YOU

Thank you so much for reading this book, I hope you've found it both enjoyable to read and useful!

We are on the cusp of a genuine digital revolution in banking services. Innovation is driven around what customers want. Investments are heavily made to create a single point of entry to all digital banking services. Systems are also being built with an eye to the future, ensuring they have the flexibility to allow them to adapt to new and emerging technologies.

The future holds yet more change. 'Big Data' insights will allow us to tailor services to different customer needs, and to offer customers vital information about their own businesses. Banks are shifting their focus from providing product functionality to information services, and this has the capacity to revolutionize our customer's financial management through digital banking.

So let's enjoy this journey together. If you want you may follow me on Twitter (@ttavlas) or visit my blog: www.digitalbankingtips.com for new tips. Also, please feel free to contact me if you have any feedback: tolga@digitalbankingtips.com